THE BIG·NOTE
WORSHIP BOOK
2ND EDITION

ISBN 978-1-5400-2368-1

HAL·LEONARD®

7777 W. BLUEMOUND RD. P.O. BOX 13819 MILWAUKEE, WI 53213

Visit Hal Leonard Online at
www.halleonard.com

CORNERSTONE

Words and Music by JONAS MYRIN,
REUBEN MORGAN, ERIC LILJERO
and EDWARD MOTE

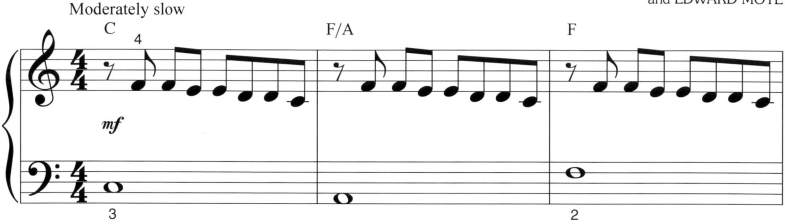

My hope is built   on   noth-ing less
When dark-ness seems   to   hide His face,

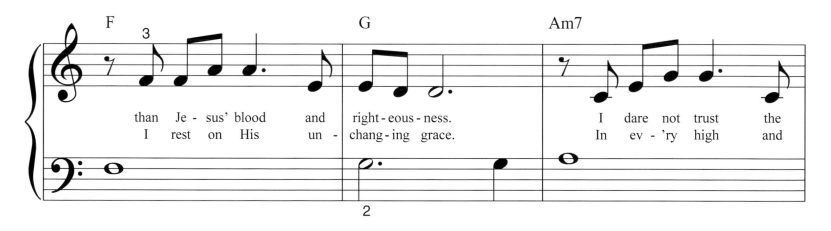

than Je-sus' blood   and   right-eous-ness.   I dare not trust   the
I rest on His   un-   chang-ing grace.   In ev-'ry high   and

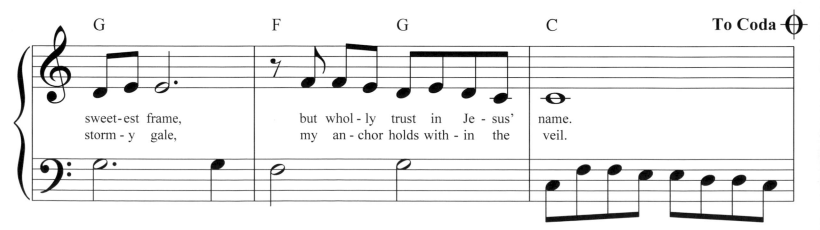

sweet-est frame,   but whol-ly trust in Je-sus'   name.
storm-y gale,   my an-chor holds with-in   the   veil.

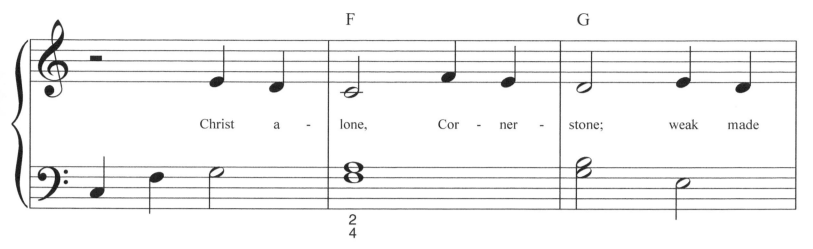

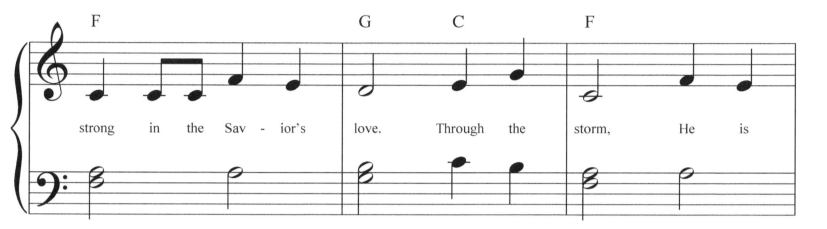

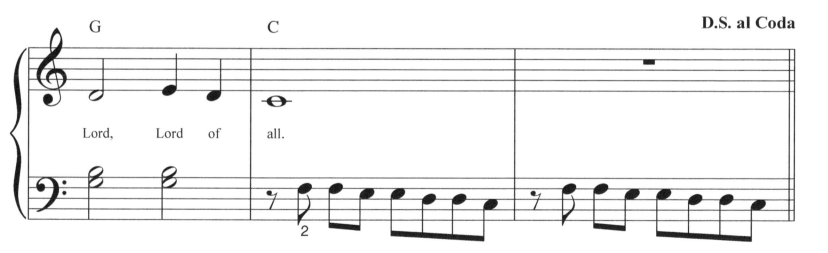

D.S. al Coda

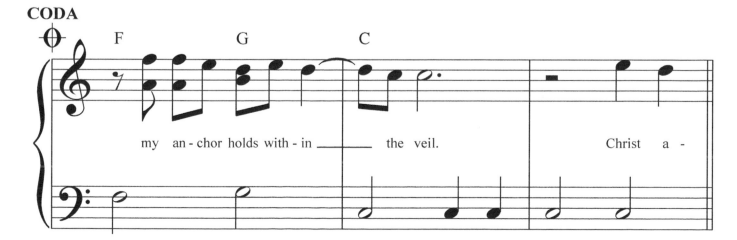

CODA

lone, Cor - ner - stone; weak made strong in the Sav - ior's love. Through the

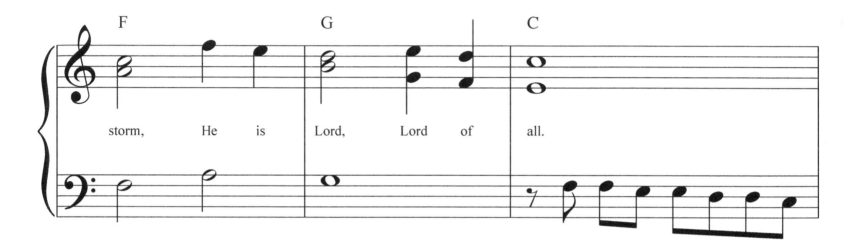

storm, He is Lord, Lord of all.

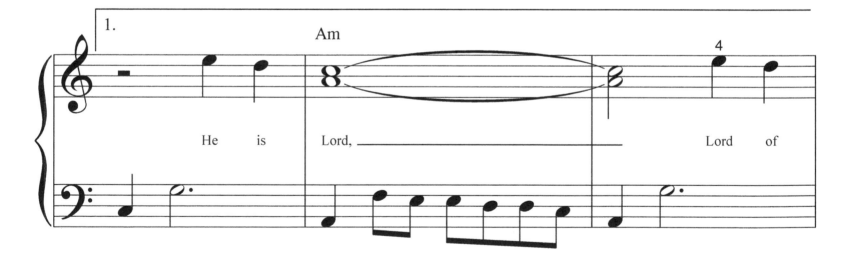

1.

He is Lord, _____ Lord of

all. _____ Christ a -

2.

AMAZING GRACE
(My Chains Are Gone)

Words by JOHN NEWTON
Traditional American Melody
Additional Words and Music by CHRIS TOMLIN
and LOUIE GIGLIO

Moderately slow

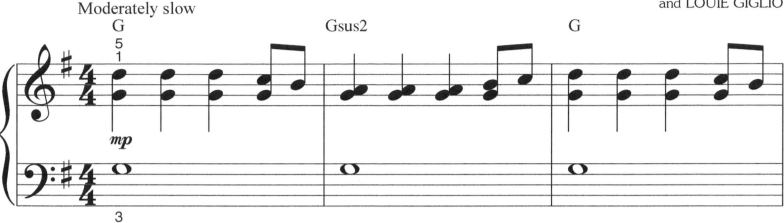

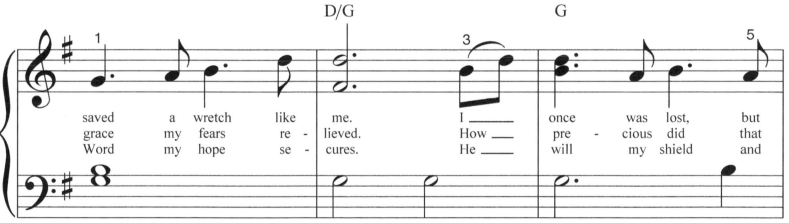

A - maz - ing grace, how sweet the sound, that
grace that taught my heart to fear, and
Lord has prom - ised good to me, and His

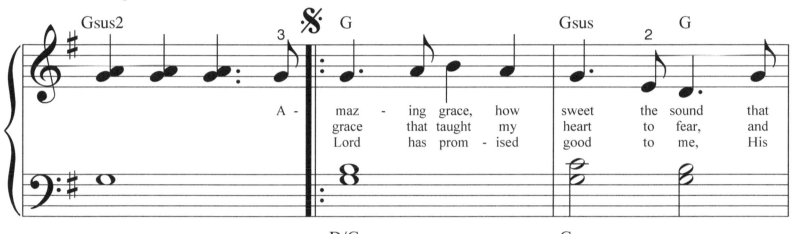

saved a wretch like me. I once was lost, but
grace my fears re - lieved. How pre - cious did that
Word my hope se - cures. He will my shield and

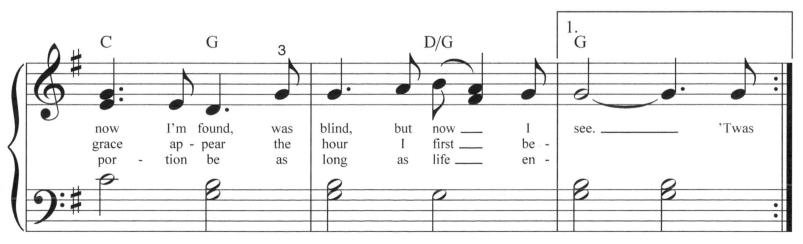

now I'm found, was blind, but now I see. 'Twas
grace ap - pear the hour I first be -
por - tion be as long as life en -

6

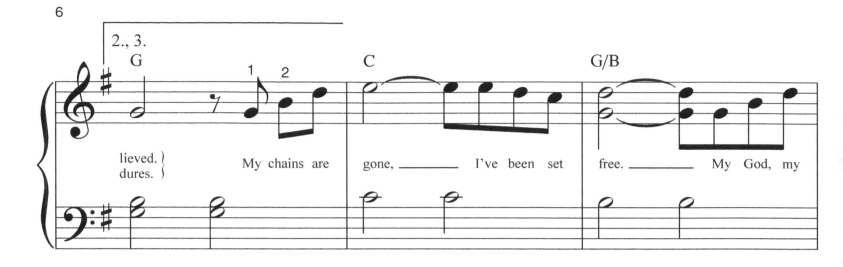

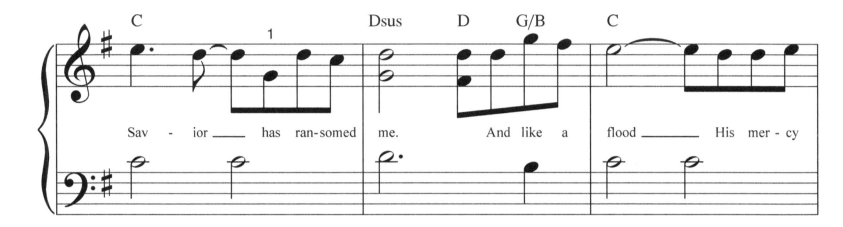

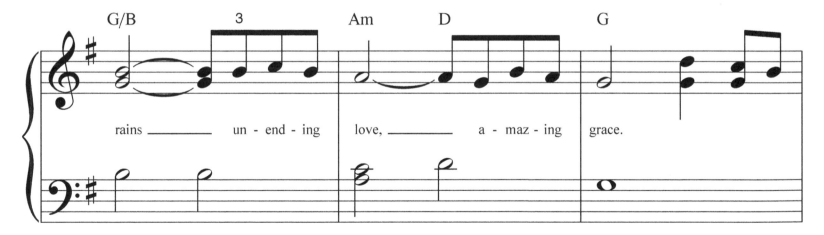

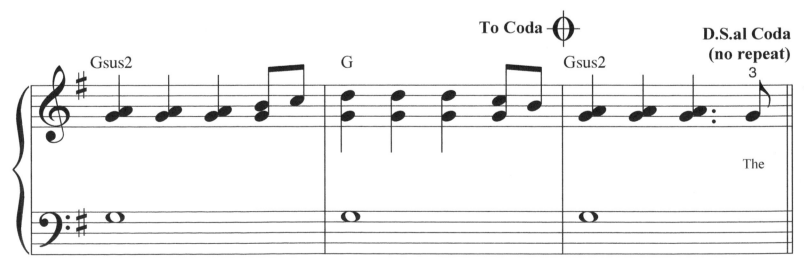

CODA

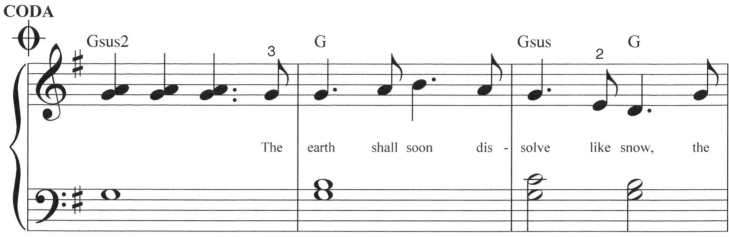

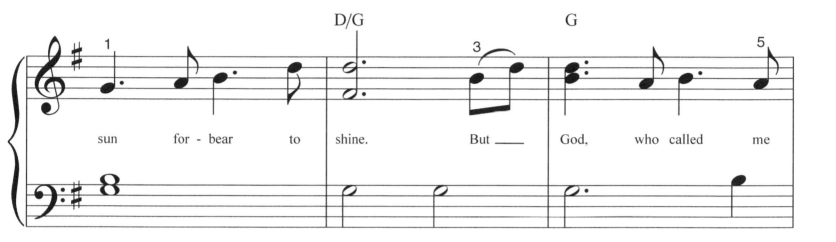

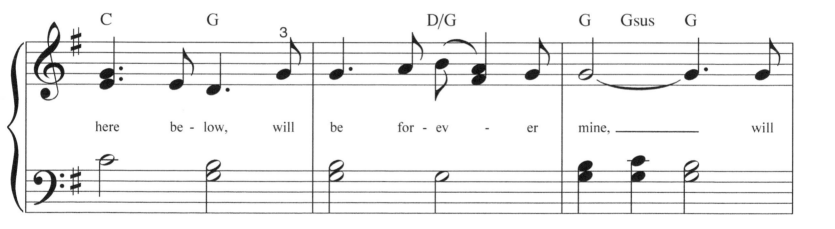

HERE I AM TO WORSHIP
(Light of the World)

Words and Music by
TIM HUGHES

Moderately slow

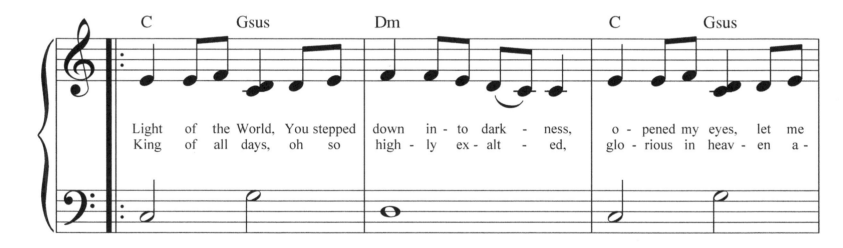

Light of the World, You stepped down in-to dark - ness,
King of all days, oh so high - ly ex-alt - ed,

o - pened my eyes, let me
glo - rious in heav - en a -

see.
bove,

Beau - ty that made this____ heart a - dore____ You,
hum - bly You came to the earth You cre - a - ted,

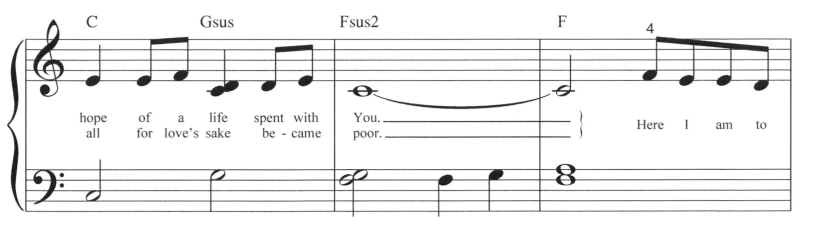

hope of a life spent with You.
all for love's sake be - came poor.

Here I am to

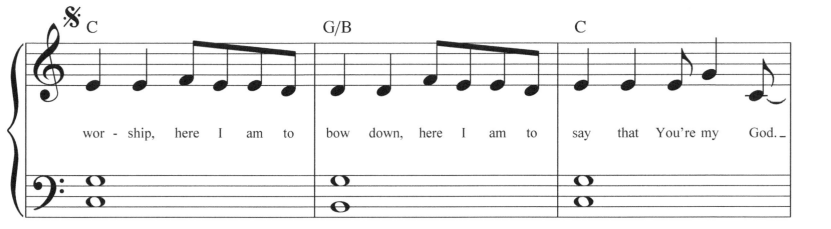

wor - ship, here I am to bow down, here I am to say that You're my God.

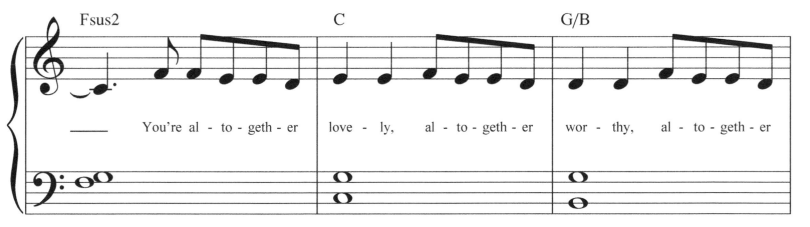

_____ You're al - to - geth - er love - ly, al - to - geth - er wor - thy, al - to - geth - er

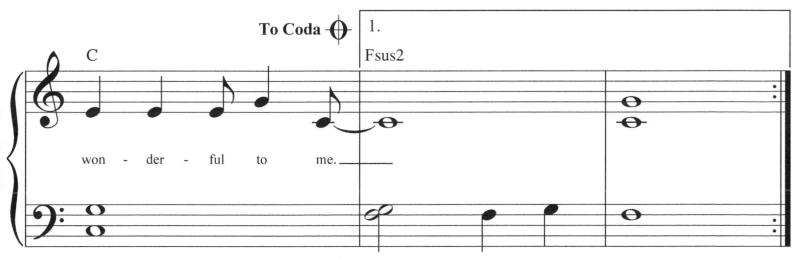

To Coda ⊕ | 1.

won - der - ful to me.

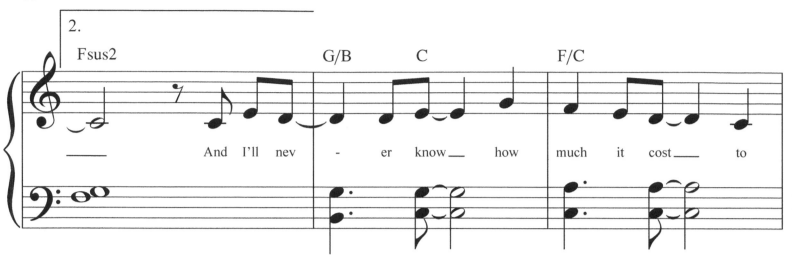

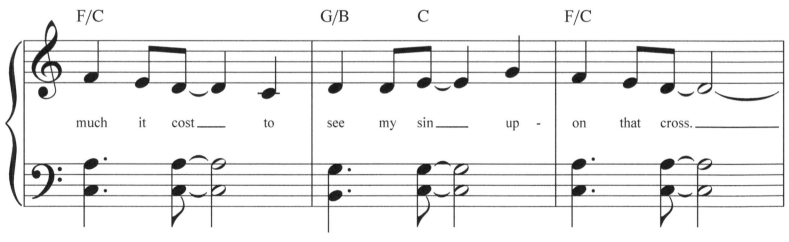

EVERLASTING GOD

Words and Music by BRENTON BROWN
and KEN RILEY

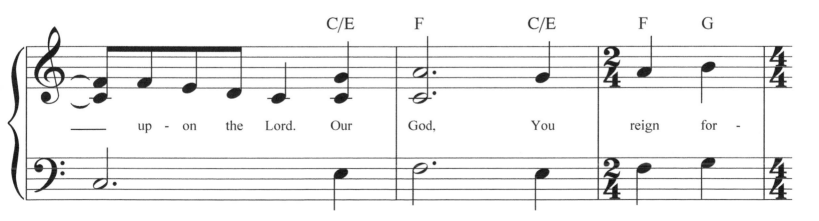

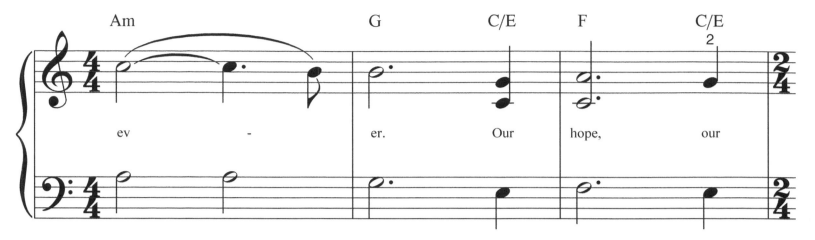

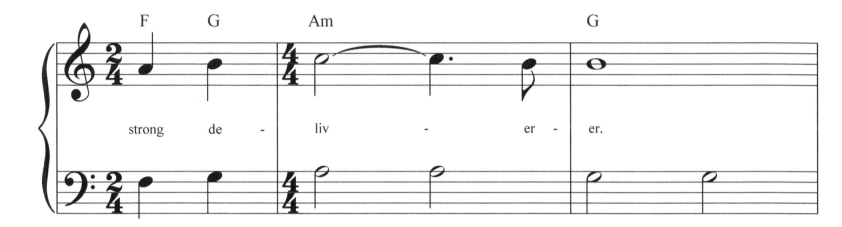

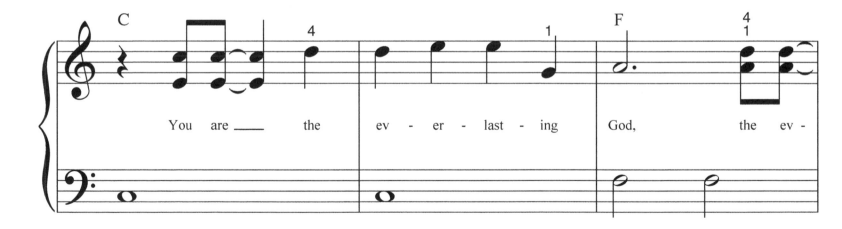

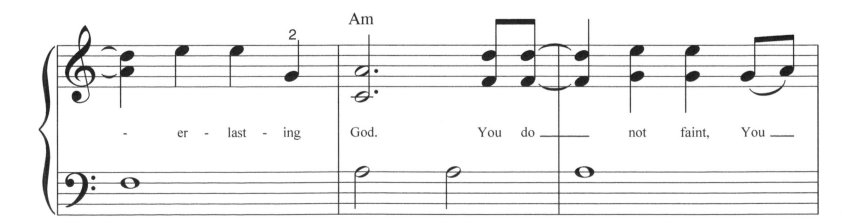

won't　　grow　　wea　-　ry.＿＿＿　　　　You're the ＿＿＿　de -

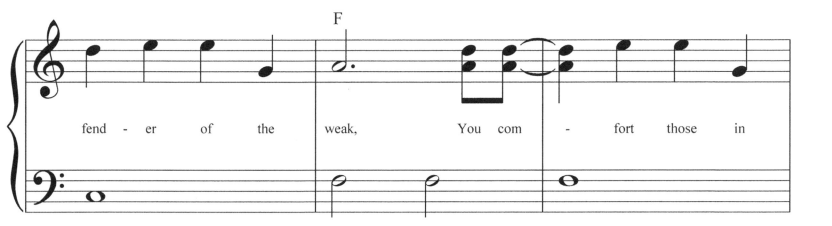

fend - er　of　the　weak,　　　You com　-　fort those　in

need,　　You lift ＿＿＿　us　up　on ＿＿＿　wings　like

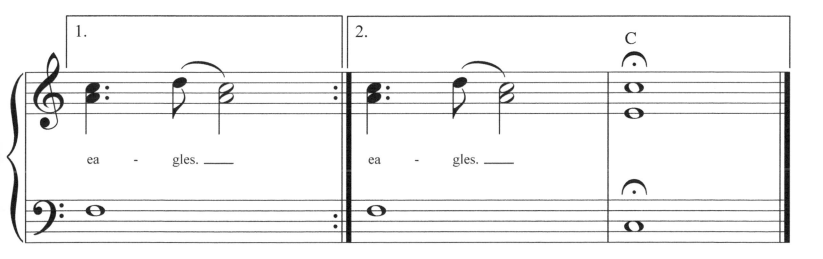

ea - gles. ＿＿＿　　　　ea - gles. ＿＿＿

GOOD GOOD FATHER

Words and Music by PAT BARRETT
and ANTHONY BROWN

I'm nev - er a - lone.
we say ____ a word.

You're a good, ____ good Fa - ther. It's who You are,

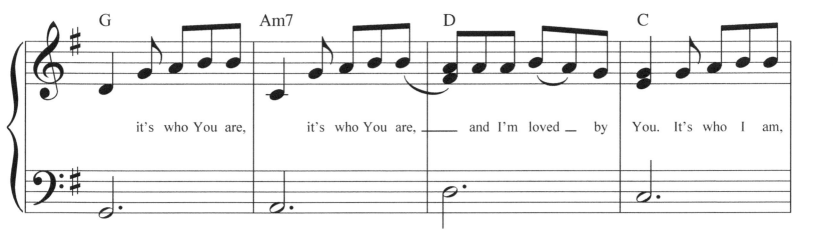

it's who You are, it's who You are, ____ and I'm loved ____ by You. It's who I am,

it's who I am, it's who I am. ____

Oh, and

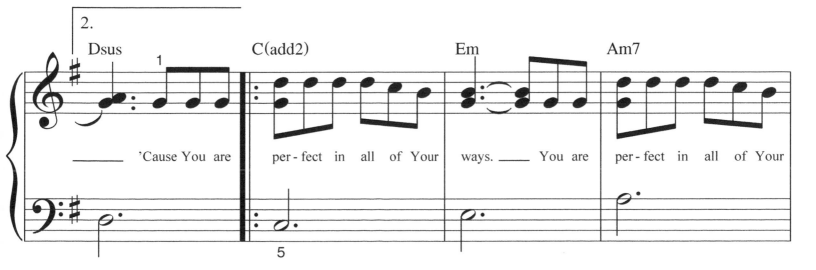

____ 'Cause You are per - fect in all of Your ways. ____ You are per - fect in all of Your

16

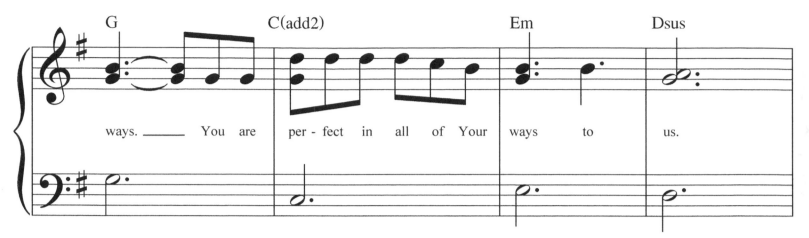

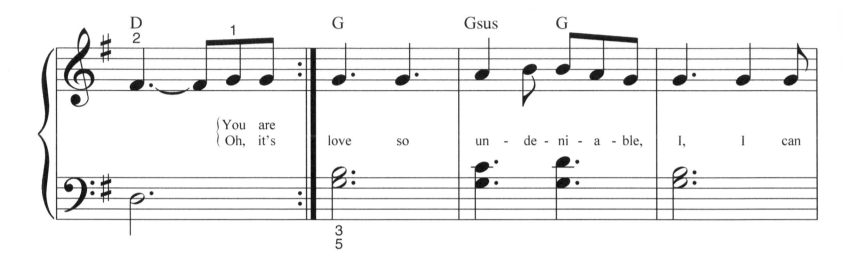

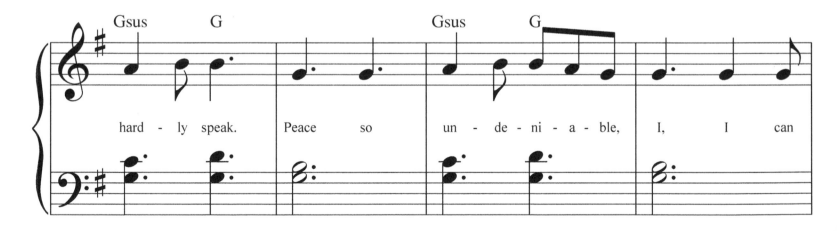

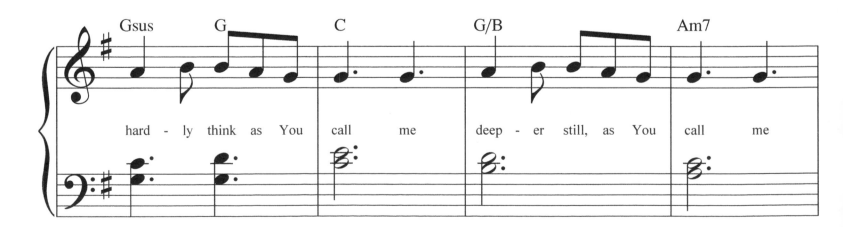

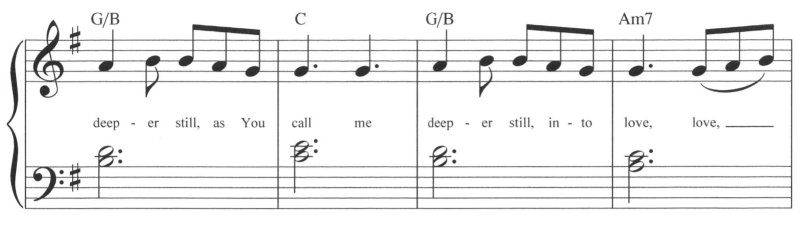

HOLY IS THE LORD

Words and Music by CHRIS TOMLIN
and LOUIE GIGLIO

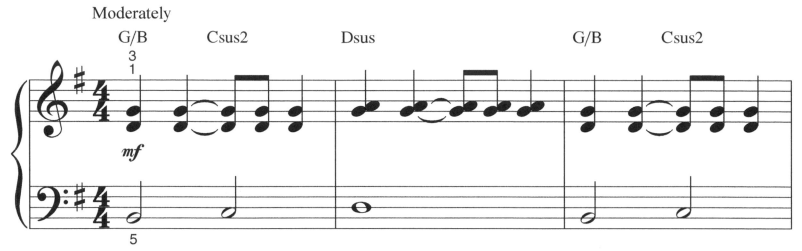

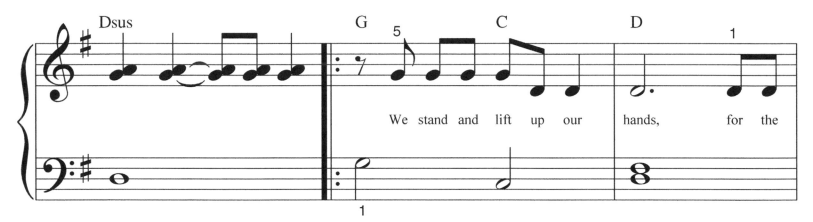

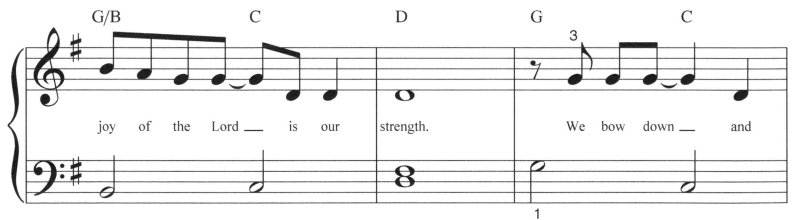

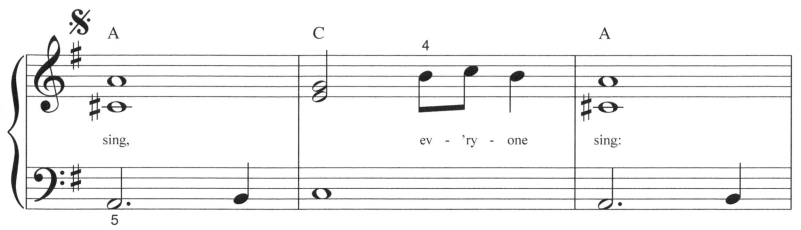

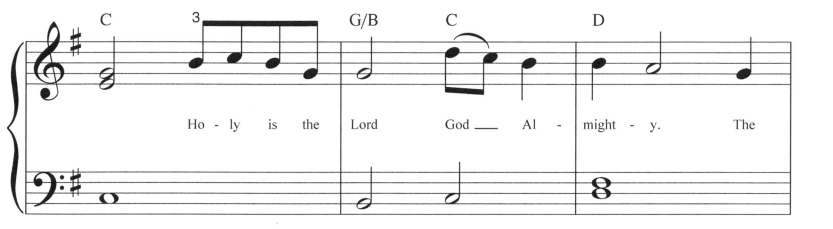

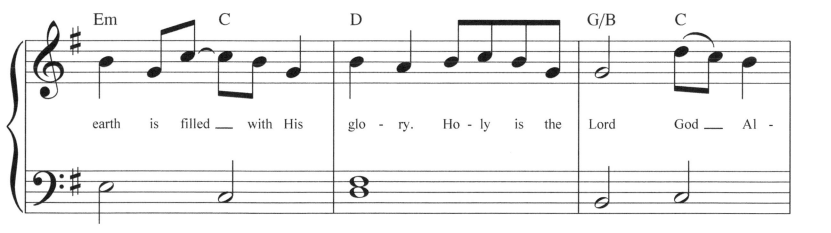

20

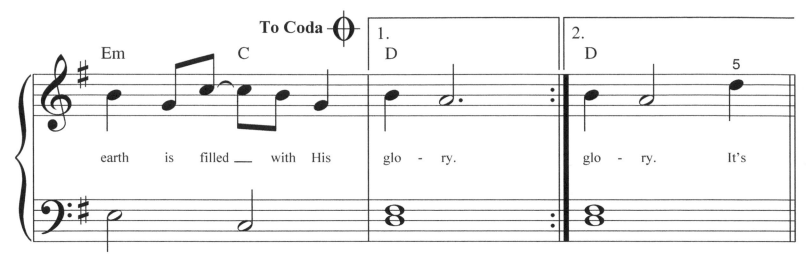

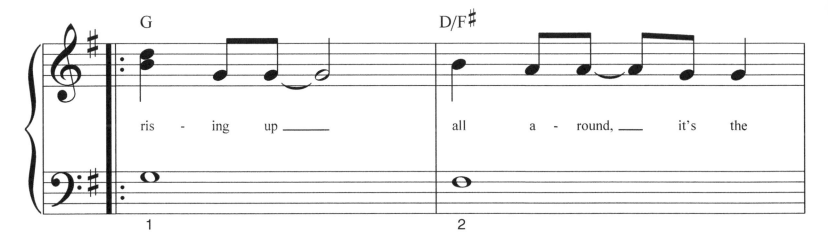

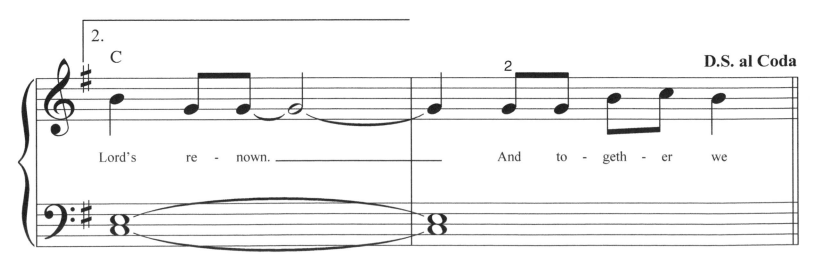

CODA

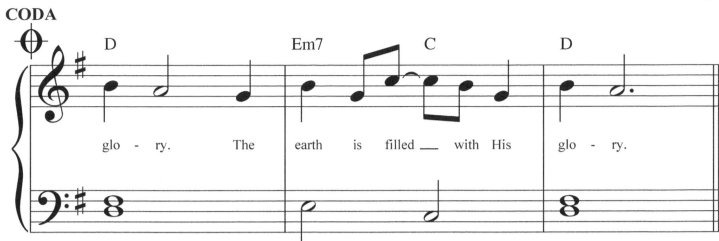

glo - ry. The earth is filled __ with His glo - ry.

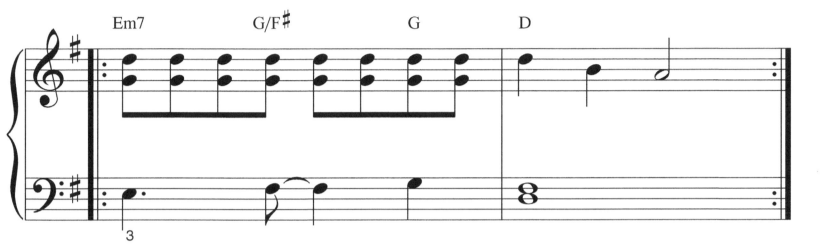

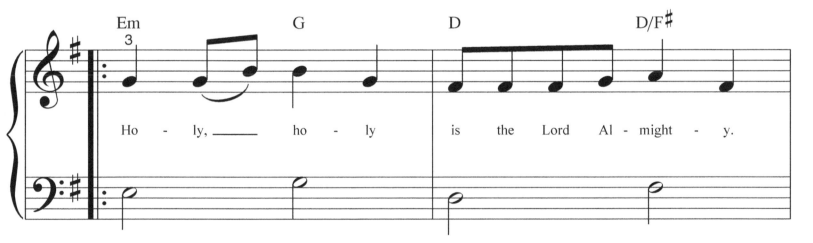

Ho - ly, __ ho - ly is the Lord Al - might - y.

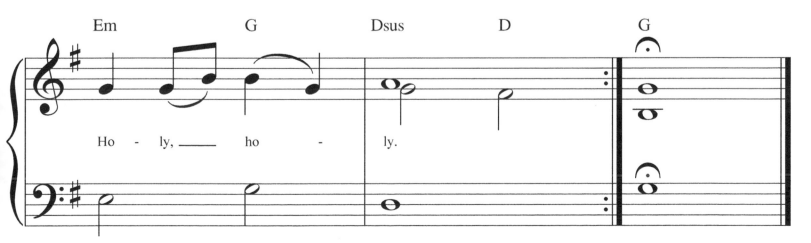

Ho - ly, __ ho - ly.

HOLY SPIRIT

Words and Music by KATIE TORWALT
and BRYAN TORWALT

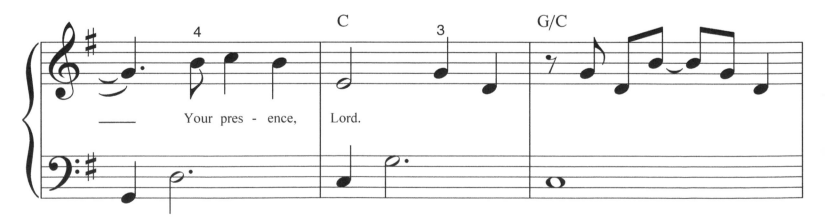

I've tast-ed and seen _____ of the sweet-est of loves, _____ where my heart be-comes free _

_____ and my shame is un - done. _____ Your pres - ence,

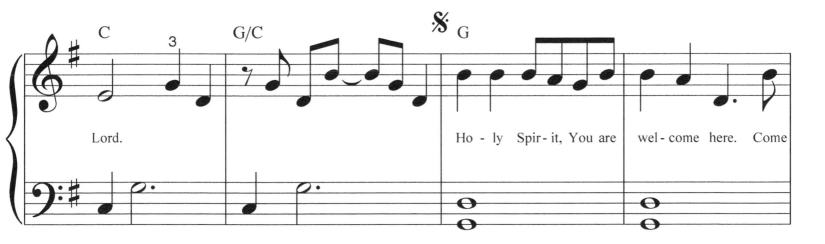

Lord. Ho - ly Spir- it, You are wel - come here. Come

flood this place and fill the at - mos - phere. Your glo - ry, God, is what our

24

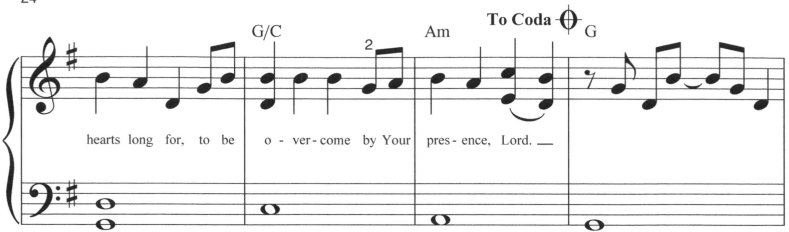

hearts long for, to be   o - ver - come by Your   pres - ence, Lord. __

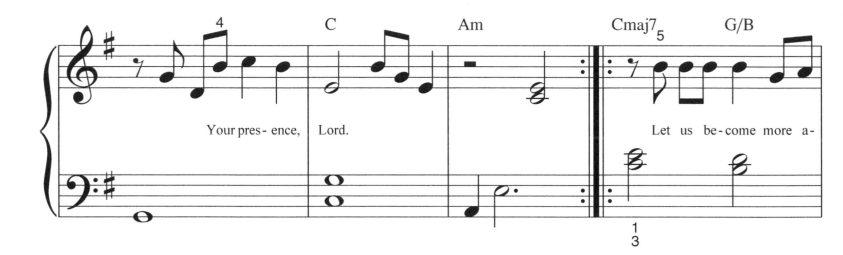

Your pres - ence,   Lord.   Let us be - come more a-

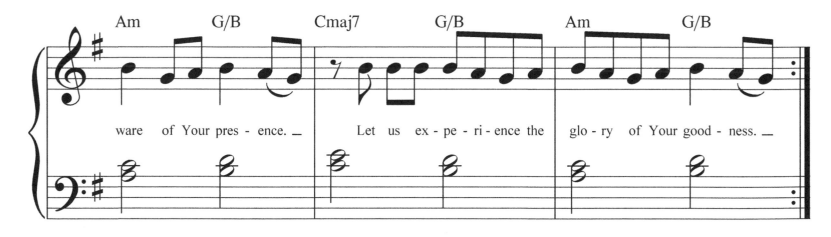

ware   of Your pres - ence. __   Let us ex - pe - ri - ence the   glo - ry   of Your good - ness. __

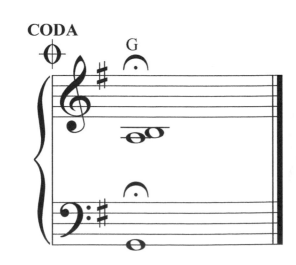

REVELATION SONG

Words and Music by
JENNIE LEE RIDDLE

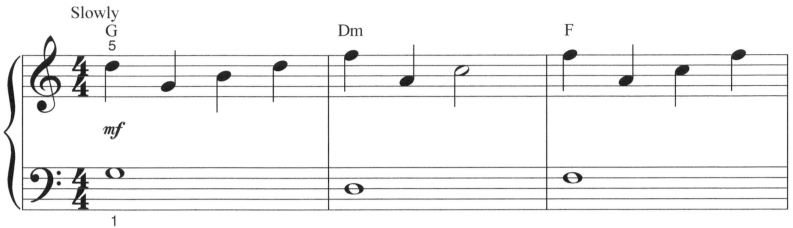

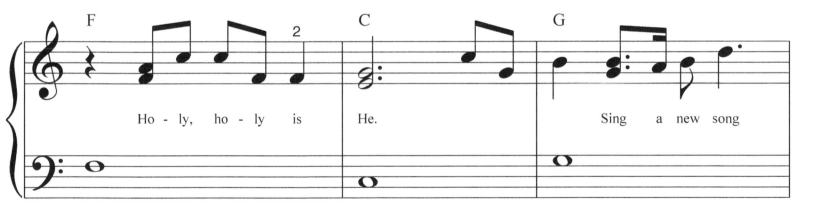

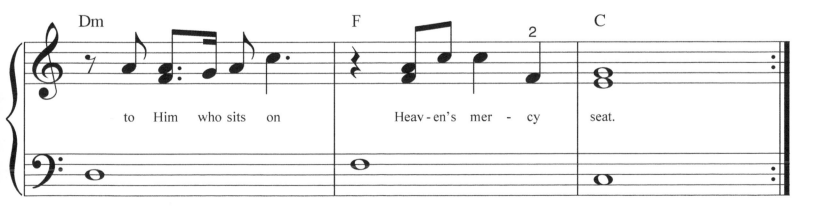

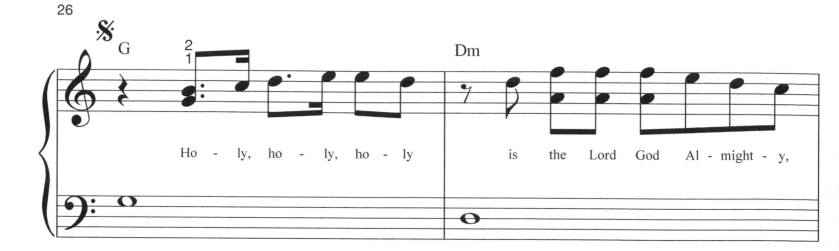

Ho - ly, ho - ly, ho - ly   is the Lord God Al - might - y,

who was and is and is to   come.   With all   cre - a - tion, I sing

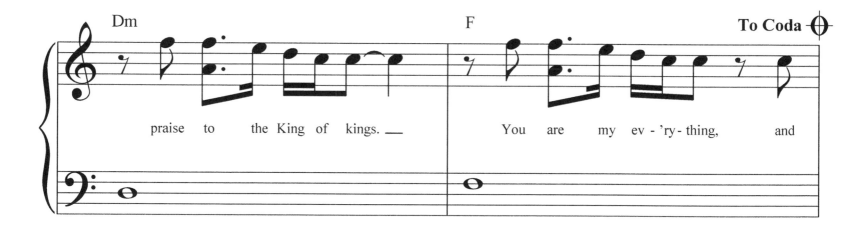

praise to   the King of kings. ___   You are   my ev - 'ry - thing,   and

I will a - dore You.   Yeah, ___ I will a -

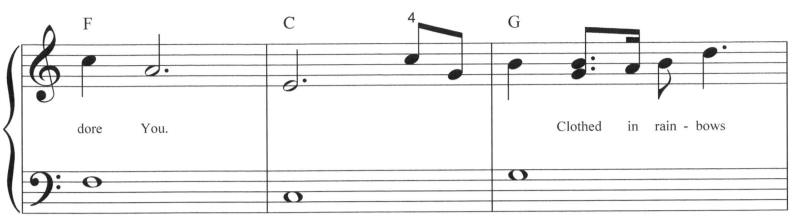

dore You.   Clothed in rain - bows

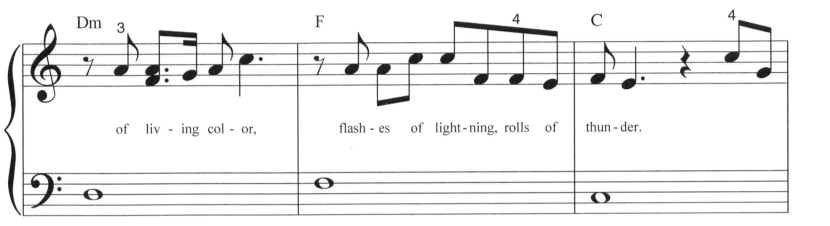

of liv - ing col - or,   flash - es   of light - ning, rolls of   thun - der.

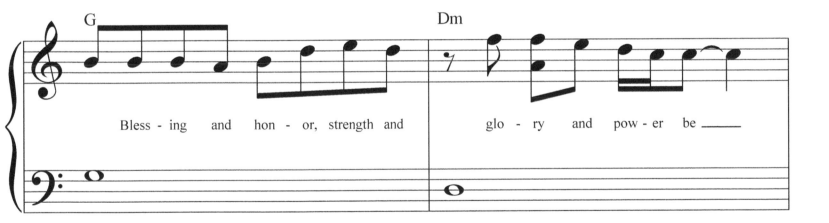

Bless - ing   and   hon - or, strength and   glo - ry   and   pow - er be _____

D.S. al Coda

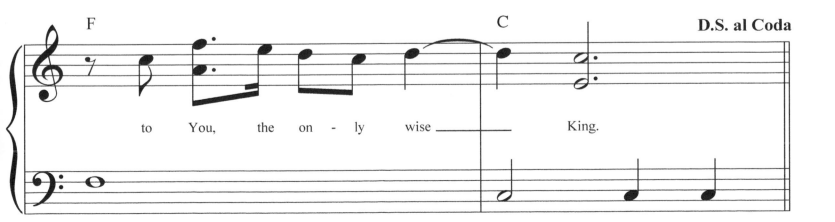

to You,   the on - ly wise _____   King.

CODA

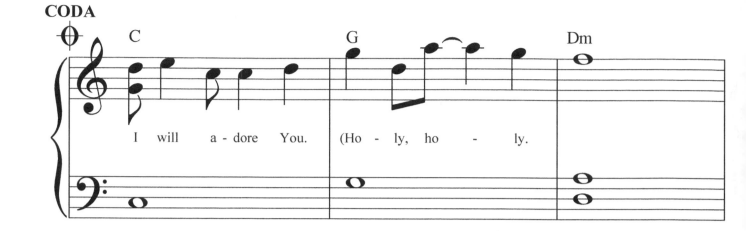

I will a-dore You. (Ho - ly, ho - ly.

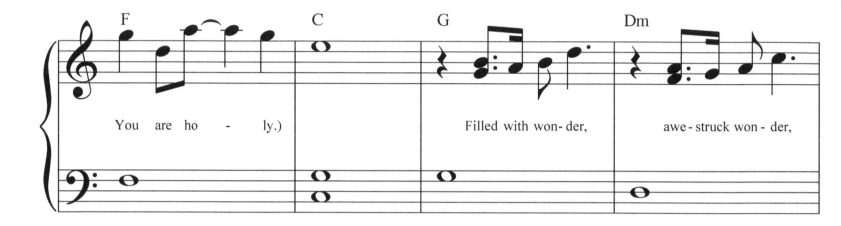

You are ho - ly.)   Filled with won- der,   awe - struck won - der,

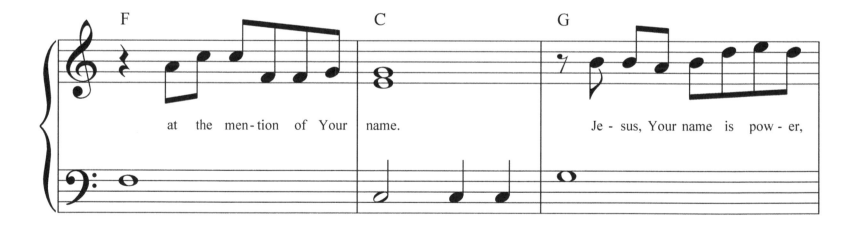

at the men-tion of Your name.   Je - sus, Your name is pow- er,

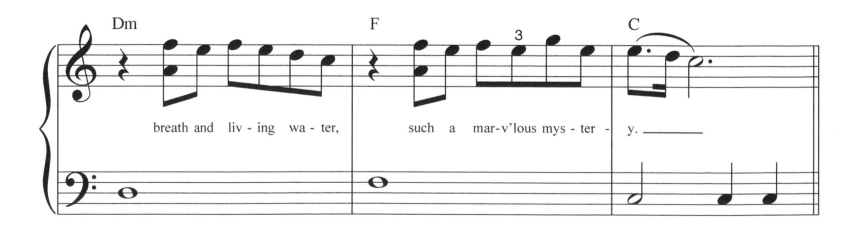

breath and liv-ing wa- ter,   such a mar-v'lous mys- ter - y.

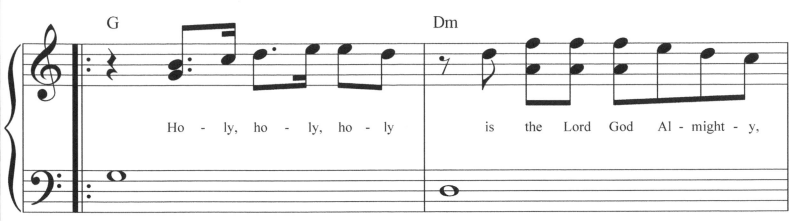

Ho - ly, ho - ly, ho - ly   is   the   Lord God   Al - might - y,

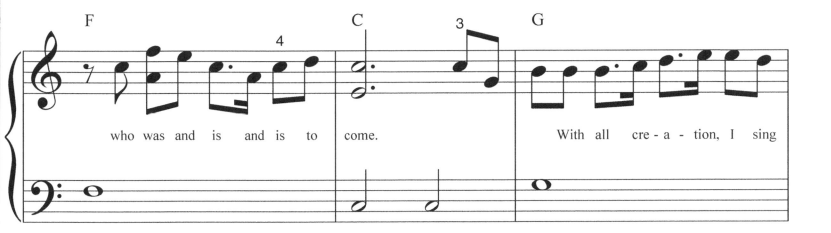

who was and is   and is to   come.   With all   cre - a - tion, I   sing

praise to   the King of kings. __   You are   my ev-'ry- thing,   and   I   will   a - dore You.

HOSANNA
(Praise Is Rising)

Words and Music by PAUL BALOCHE
and BRENTON BROWN

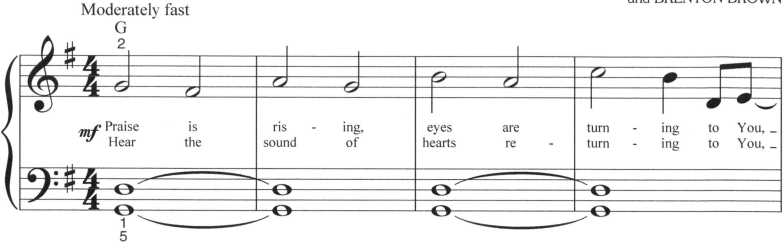

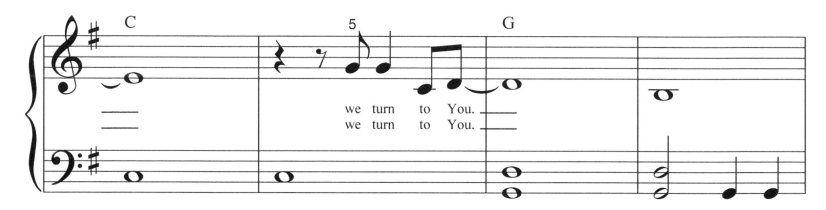

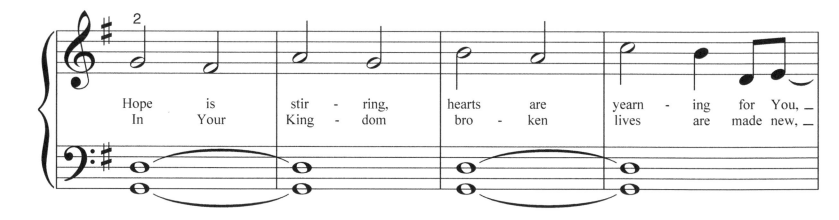

'Cause when we see ___ You, we find strength to face the day.

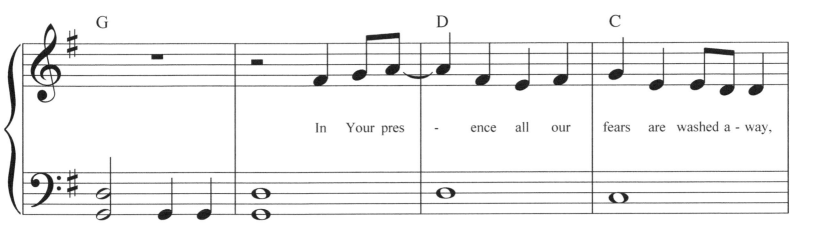

In Your pres - ence all our fears are washed a - way,

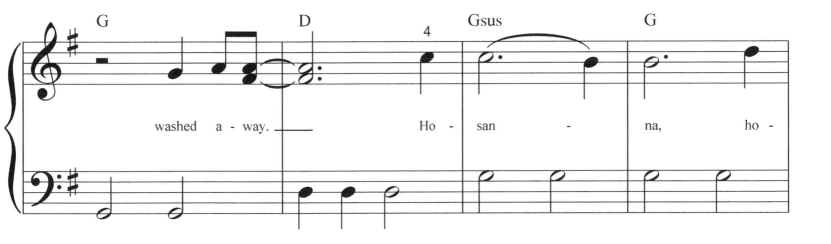

washed a - way. ___ Ho - san - na, ho -

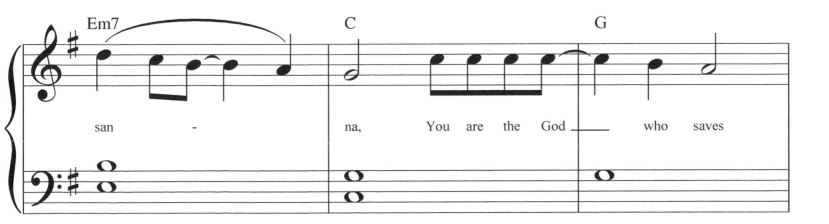

san - na, You are the God ___ who saves

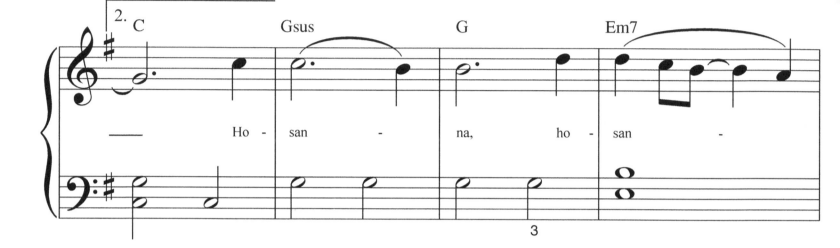

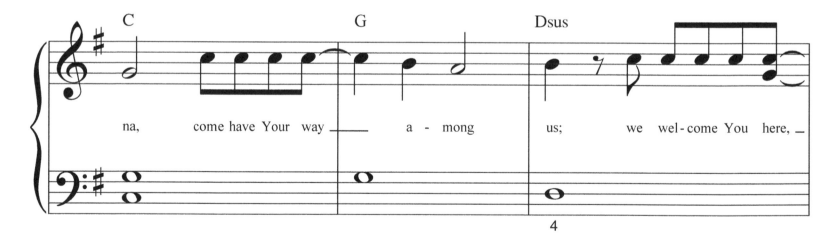

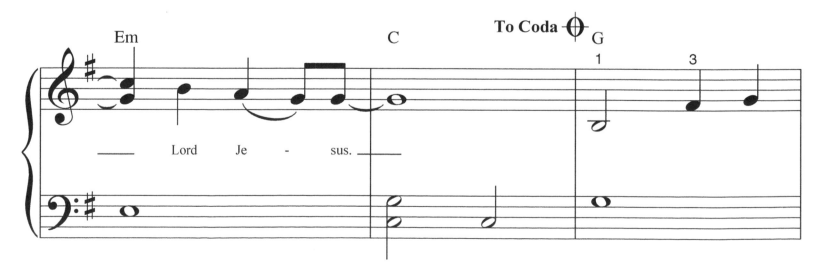

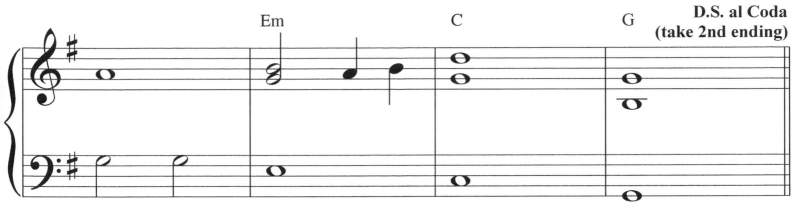

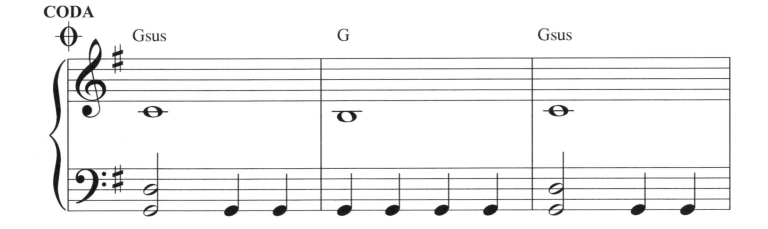

Ho - san - - na, ho - san -

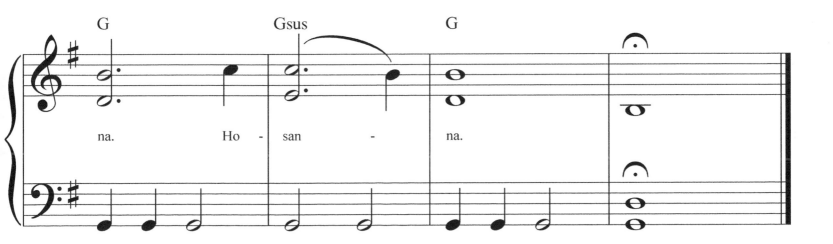

na. Ho - san - na.

HOW GREAT IS OUR GOD

Words and Music by CHRIS TOMLIN,
JESSE REEVES and ED CASH

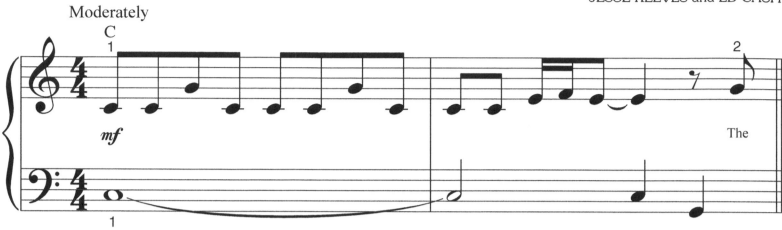

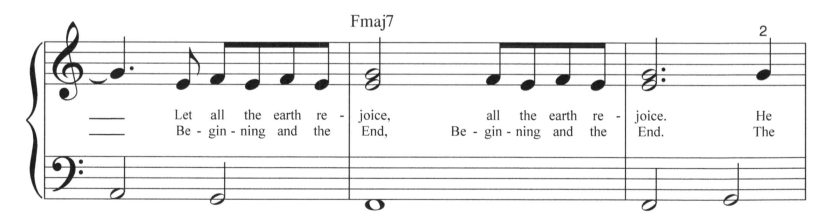

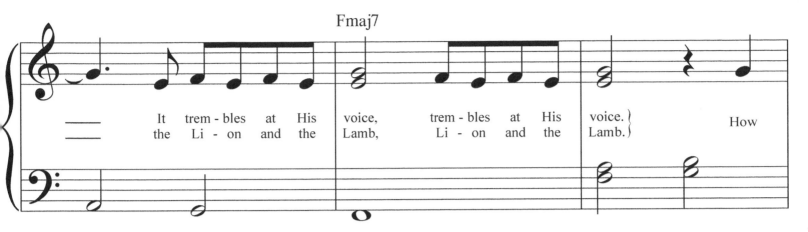

It trem - bles at His voice, trem - bles at His voice.
the Li - on and the Lamb, Li - on and the Lamb.

How

great is our God! Sing with me: How great is our

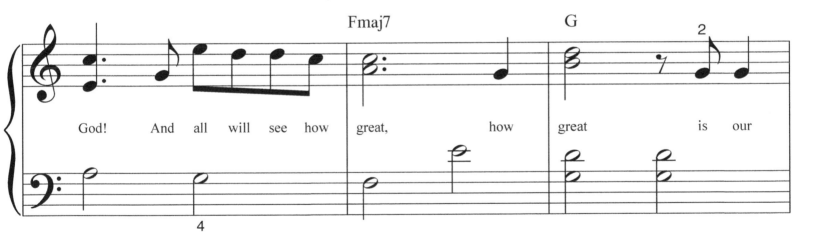

God! And all will see how great, how great is our

God!

1.

2.

Name   a - bove ___   all   names,   wor - thy of ___   all

praise.   My   heart   will   sing: _____   How

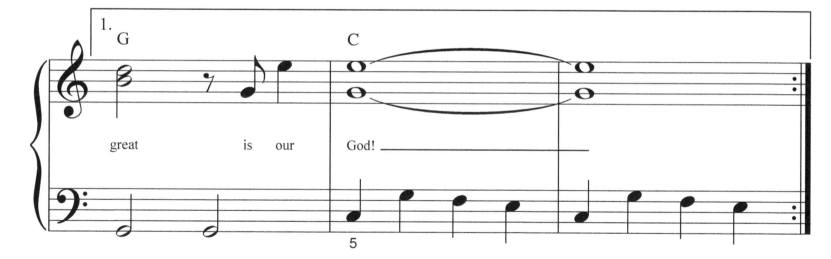

great   is   our   God! _____

great   is   our   God! _____

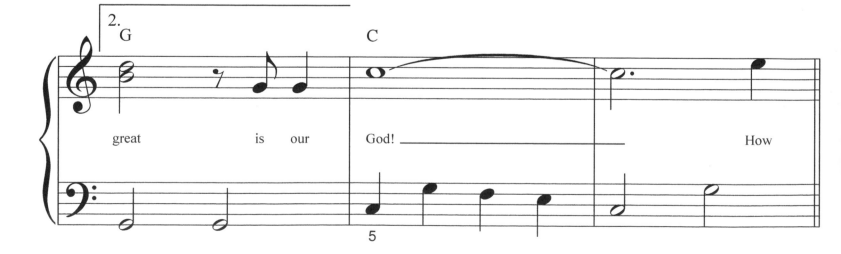

great   is   our   God! _____   How

great   is   our   God!   How

2

Am7   4   F

great   is   our   God!   How   great,   how

1.   G   C   5

great _____   is   our   God! _____   How

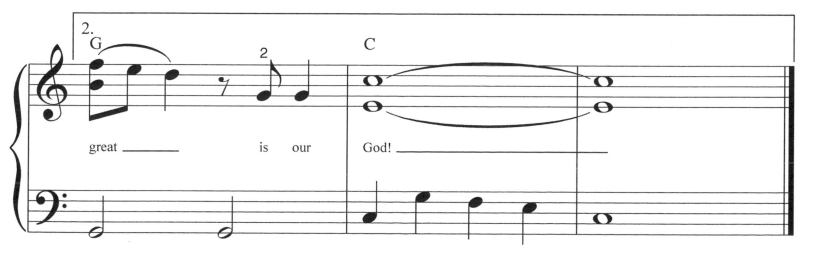

2.   G   2   C

great _____   is   our   God! _____

I GIVE YOU MY HEART

Words and Music by
REUBEN MORGAN

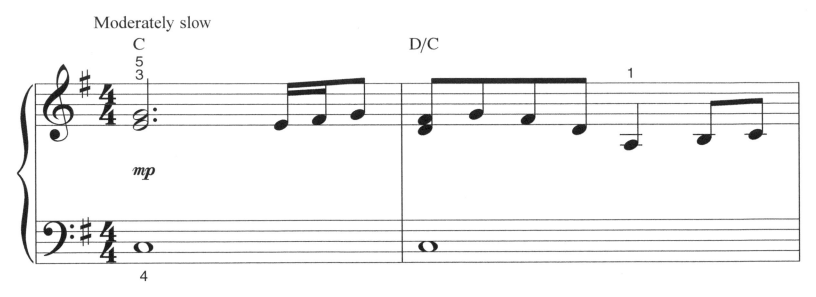

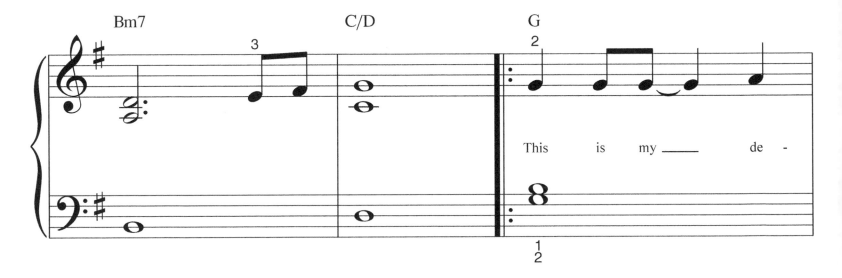

This is my ___ de -

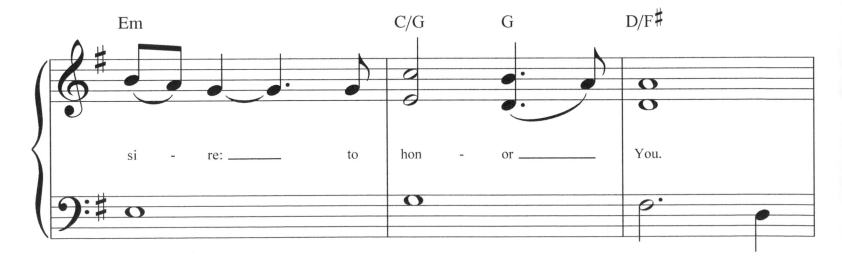

si - re: ___ to hon - or ___ You.

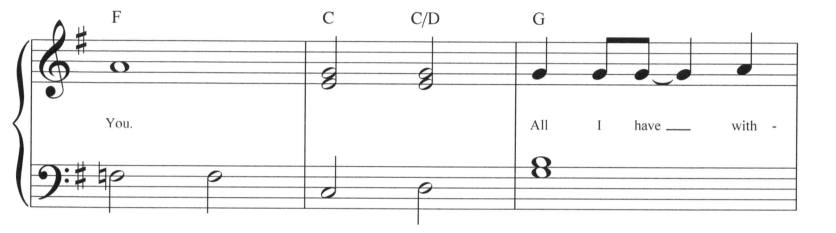

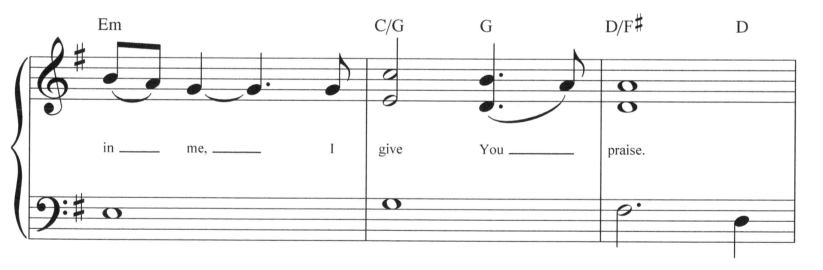

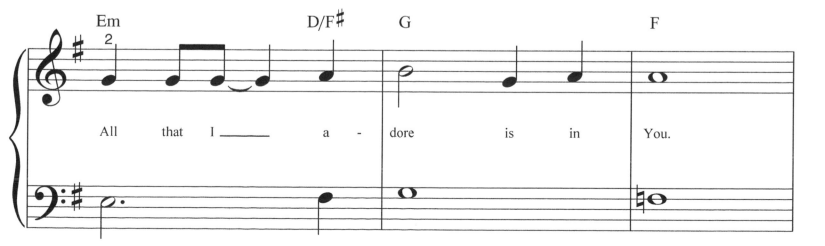

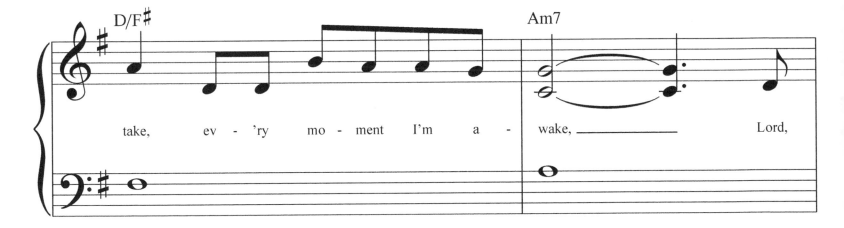

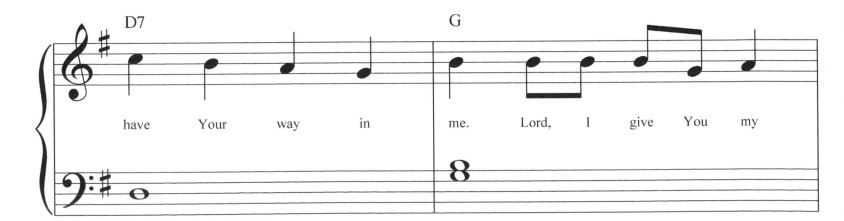

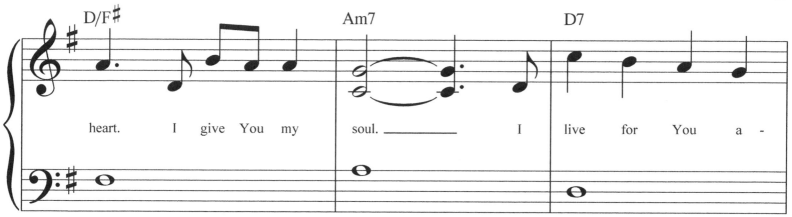

heart. I give You my soul. _____ I live for You a-

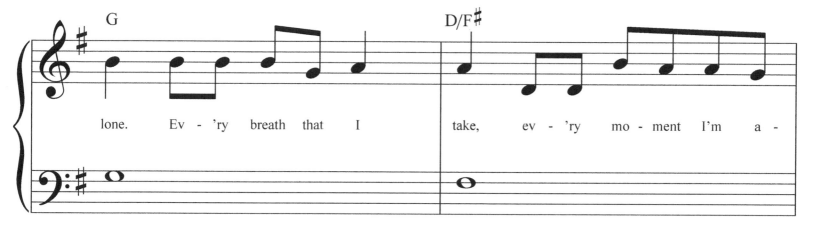

lone. Ev - 'ry breath that I take, ev - 'ry mo - ment I'm a-

wake, _____ Lord, have Your way in me.

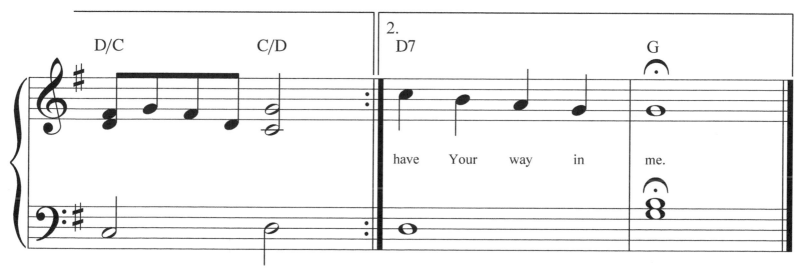

have Your way in me.

IN CHRIST ALONE

Words and Music by KEITH GETTY
and STUART TOWNEND

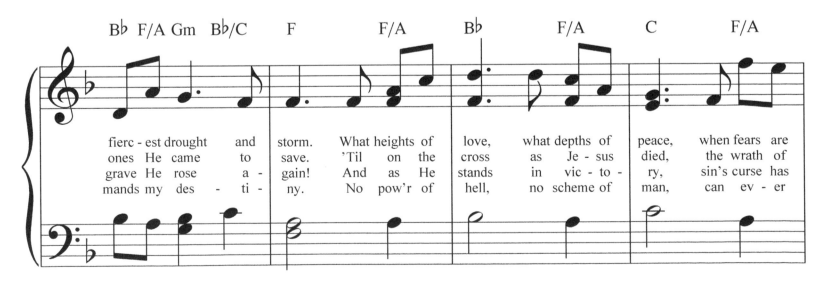

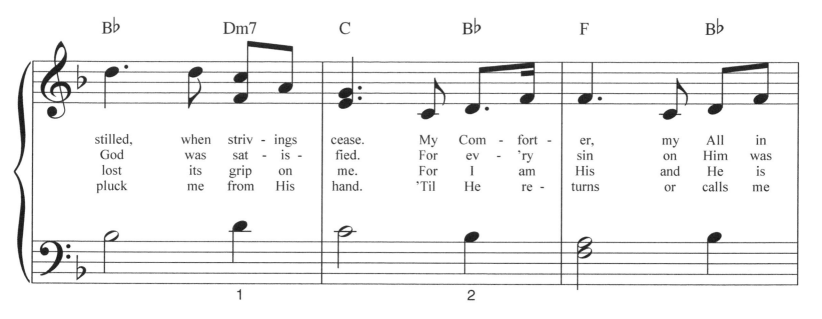

stilled, when striv - ings cease. My Com - fort - er, my All in
God was sat - is - fied. For ev - 'ry sin on Him was
lost its grip on me. For I am His and He is
pluck me from His hand. 'Til He re - turns or calls me

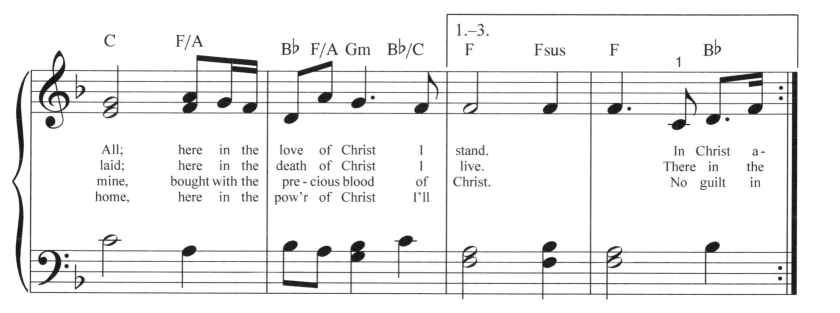

All; here in the love of Christ I stand. In Christ a -
laid; here in the death of Christ I live. There in the
mine, bought with the pre - cious blood of Christ. No guilt in
home, here in the pow'r of Christ I'll

stand! *rit.*

LORD, I NEED YOU

Words and Music by JESSE REEVES,
KRISTIAN STANFILL, MATT MAHER,
CHRISTY NOCKELS and DANIEL CARSON

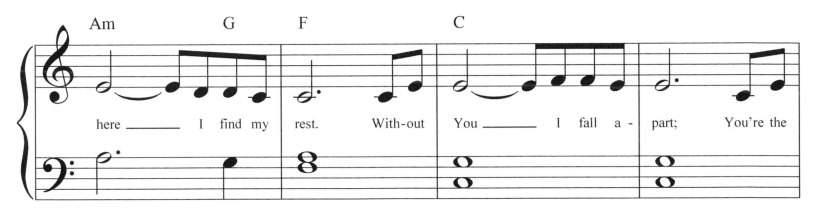

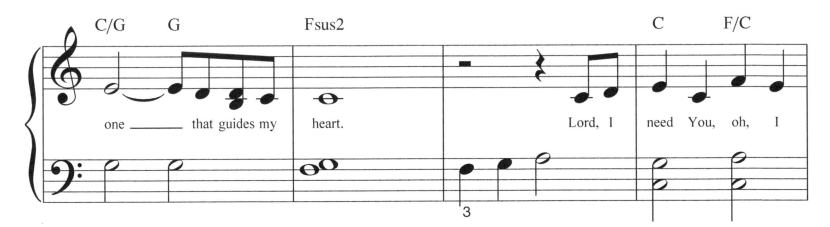

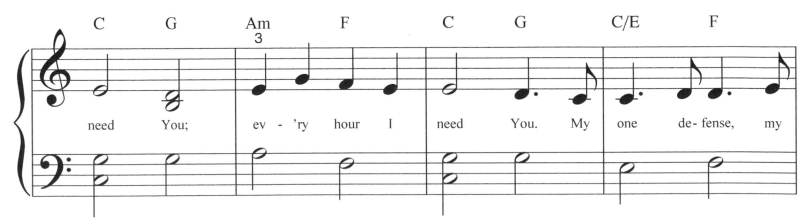

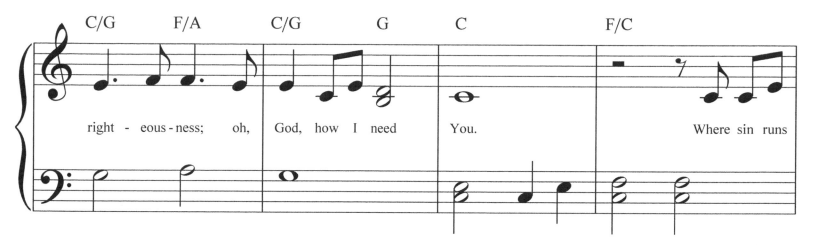

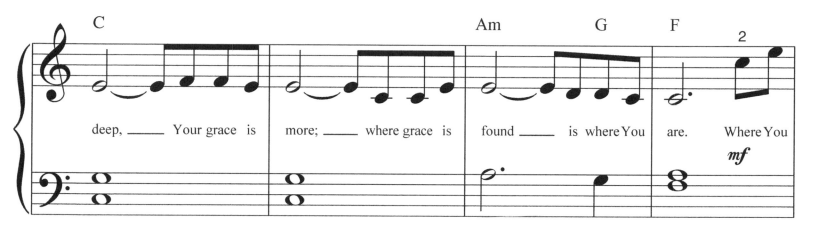

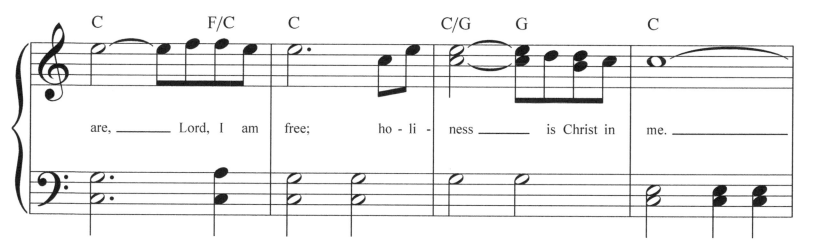

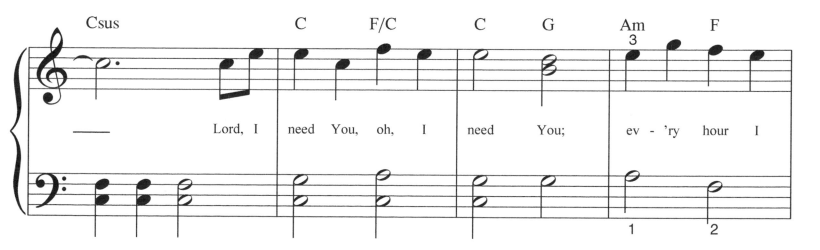

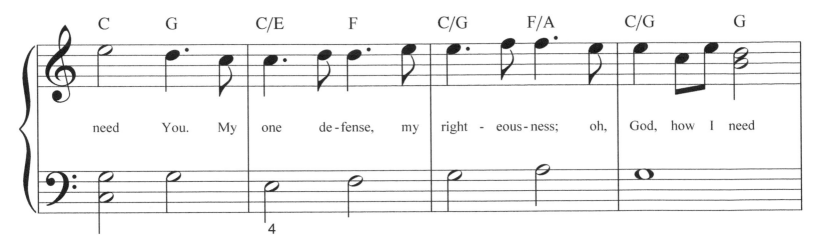

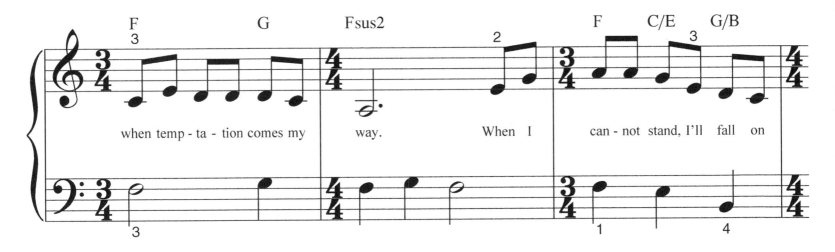

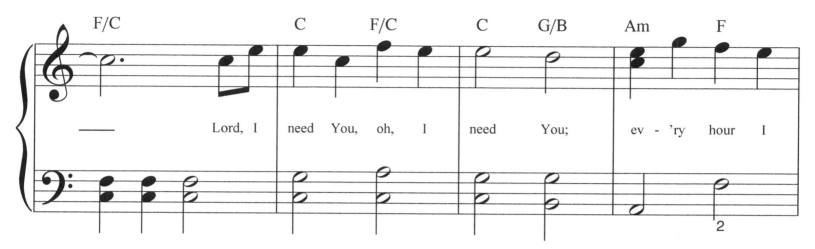

F/C   C   F/C   C   G/B   Am   F

— Lord, I need You, oh, I need You; ev-'ry hour I

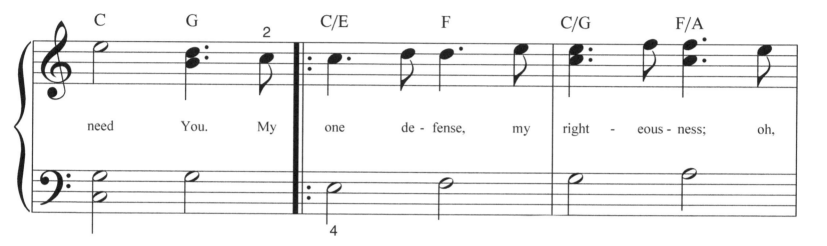

C   G   C/E   F   C/G   F/A

need You. My one de-fense, my right-eous-ness; oh,

C/G   G   1. C   2. C

God, how I need You. You're my You. ___ My

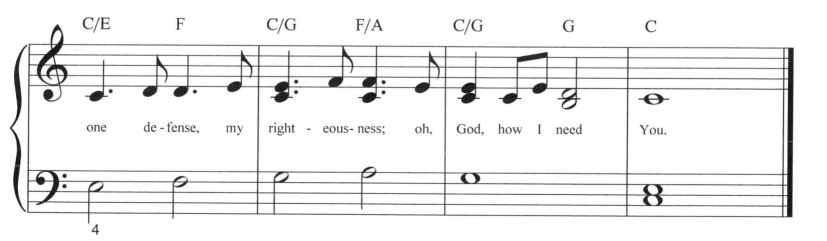

C/E   F   C/G   F/A   C/G   G   C

one de-fense, my right-eous-ness; oh, God, how I need You.

MIGHTY TO SAVE

Words and Music by BEN FIELDING
and REUBEN MORGAN

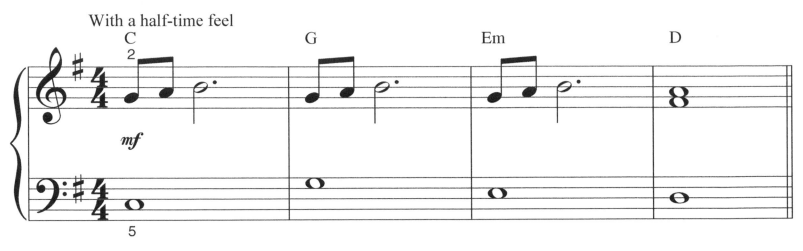

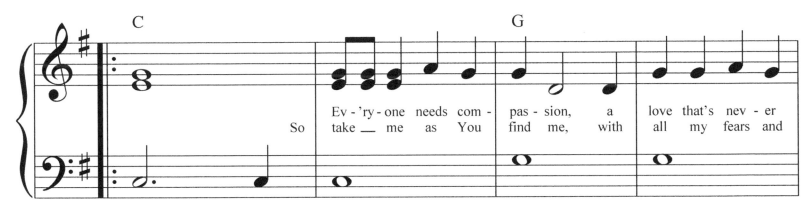

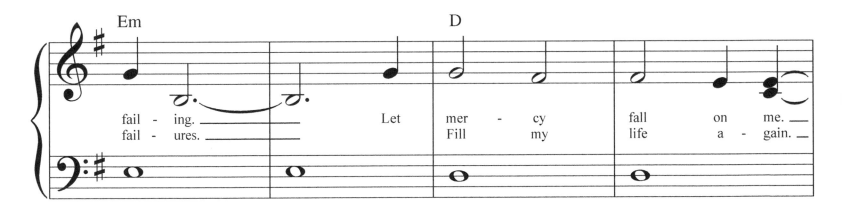

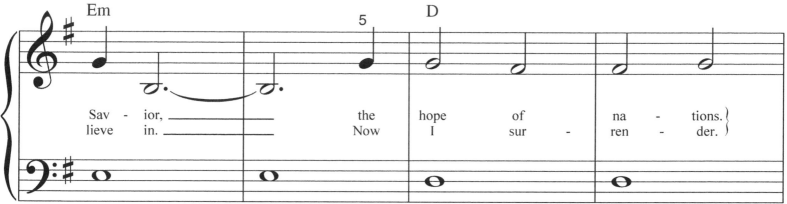

Sav - ior, _____ the hope of na - tions.
lieve in. _____ Now I of sur - ren - der.

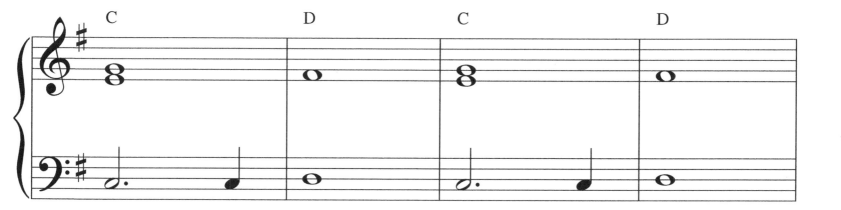

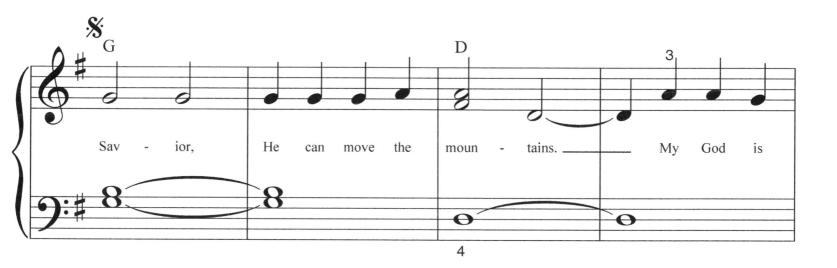

Sav - ior, He can move the moun - tains. _____ My God is

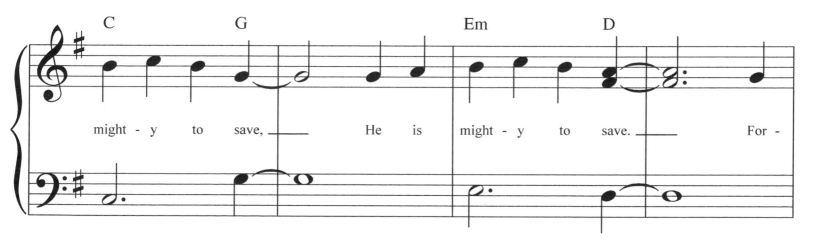

might - y to save, _____ He is might - y to save. _____ For -

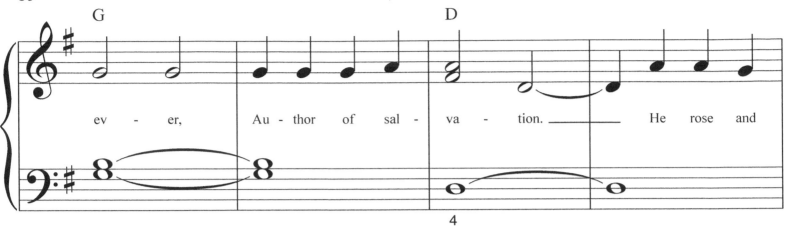

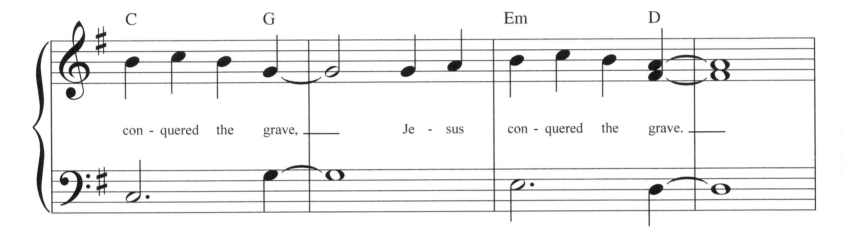

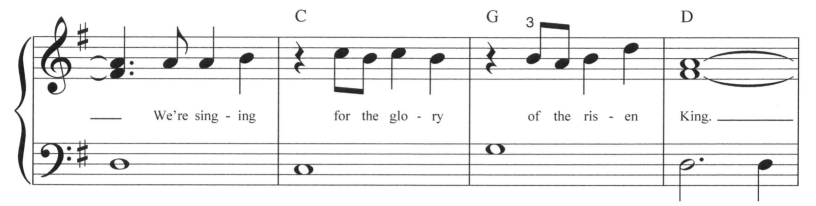

We're sing - ing · for the glo - ry · of the ris - en · King. _____

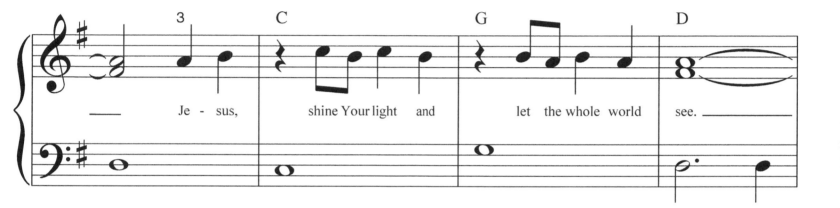

_____ Je - sus, · shine Your light and · let the whole world · see. _____

_____ We're sing - ing · for the glo - ry · of the ris - en

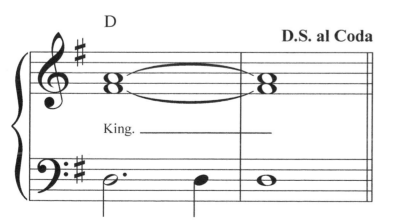

D.S. al Coda

King. _____

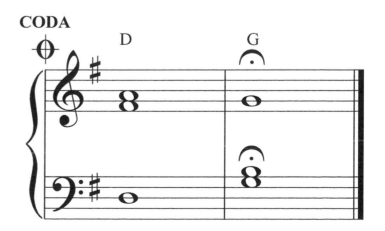

CODA

OPEN THE EYES OF MY HEART

Words and Music by
PAUL BALOCHE

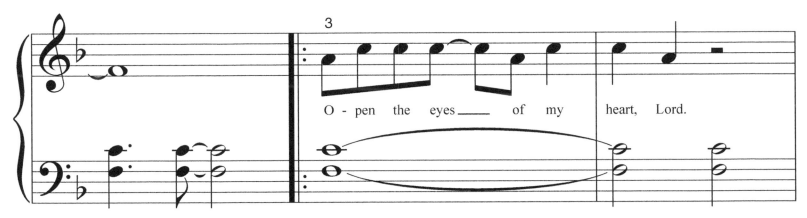

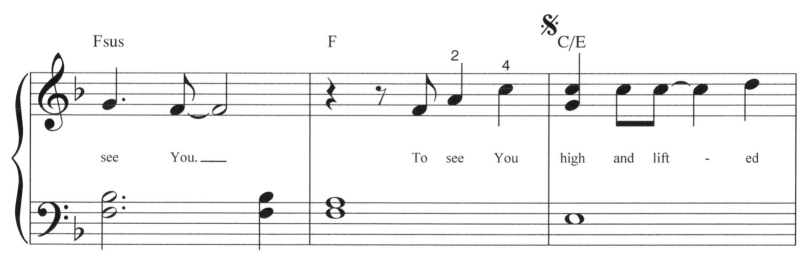

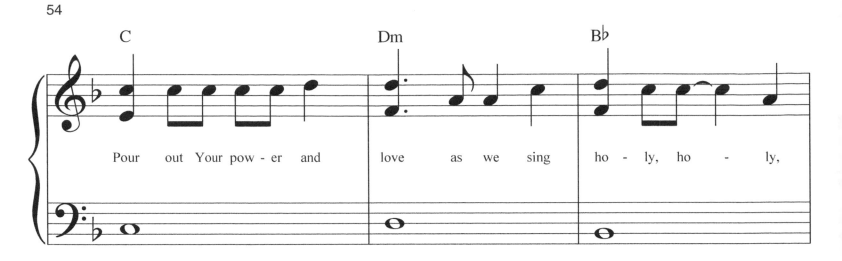

Pour out Your pow - er and love as we sing ho - ly, ho - ly,

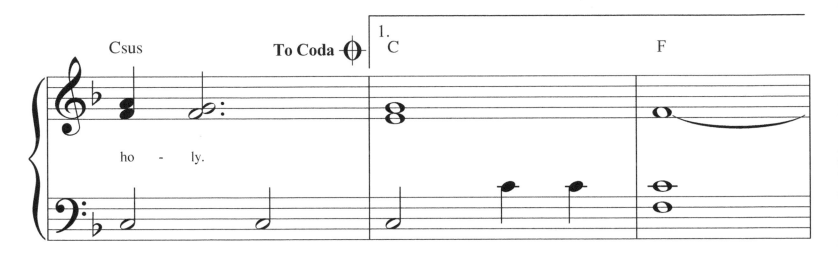

ho - ly.

To Coda ⊕

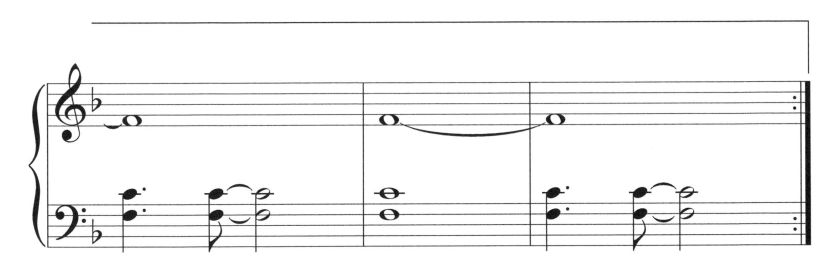

D.S. al Coda

To see You

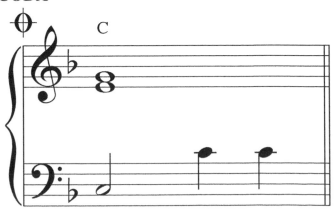

CODA

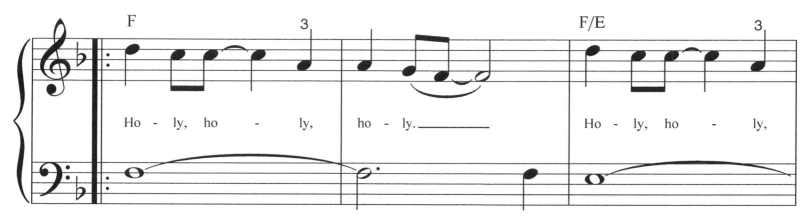

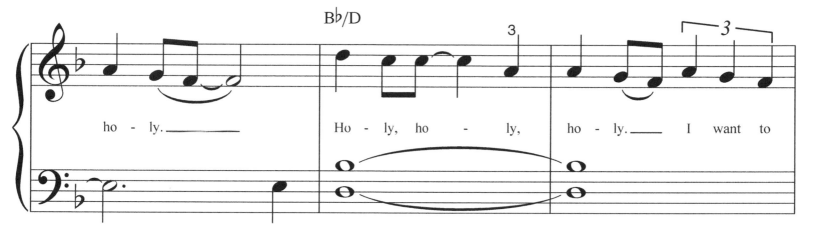

OUR GOD

Words and Music by JONAS MYRIN,
CHRIS TOMLIN, MATT REDMAN
and JESSE REEVES

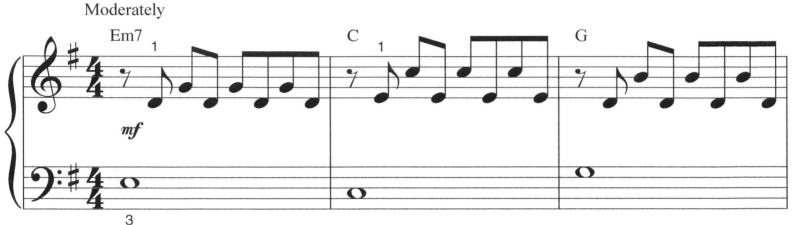

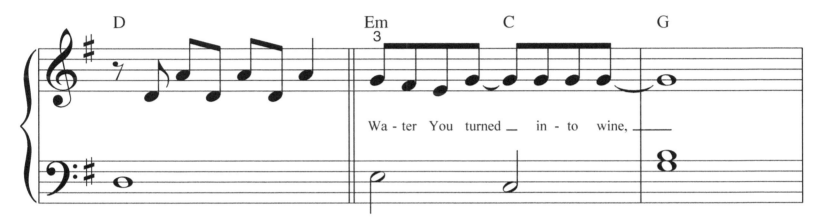

Wa - ter You turned ___ in - to wine, ___

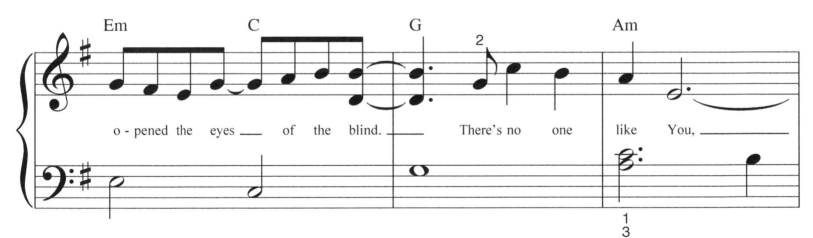

o - pened the eyes ___ of the blind. ___ There's no one like You, ___

___ none like You. ___

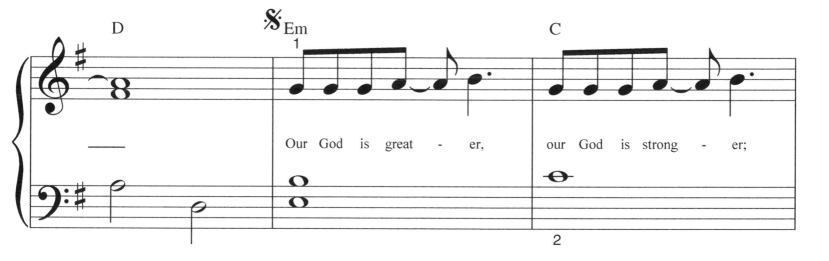

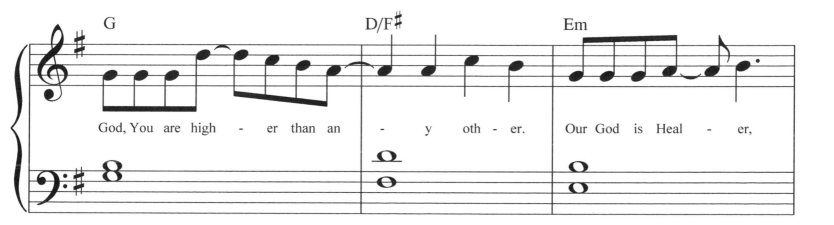

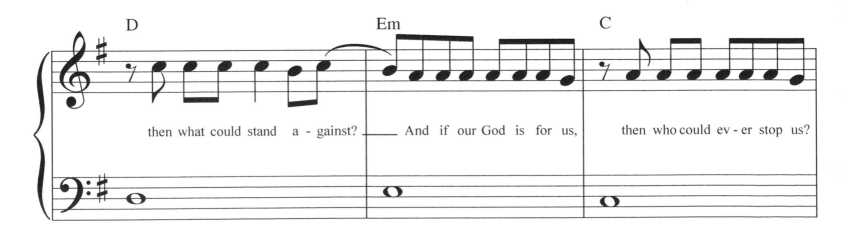

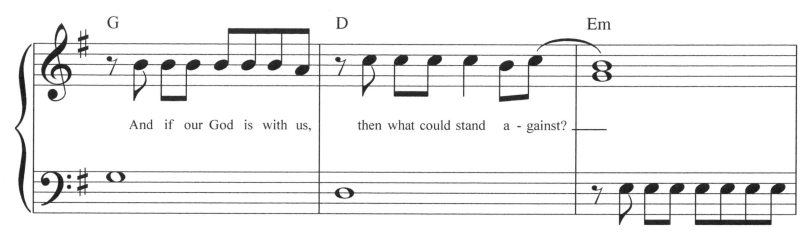

And if our God is with us, then what could stand a - gainst? ___

Then what could stand a - gainst? _

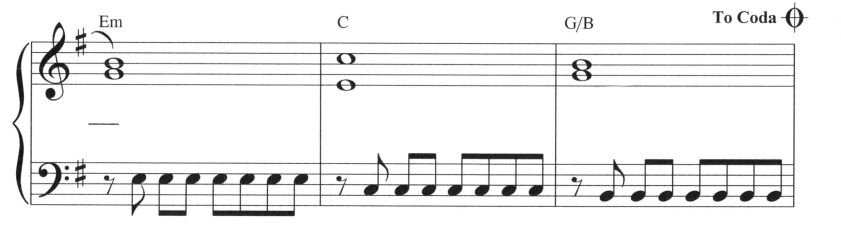

To Coda

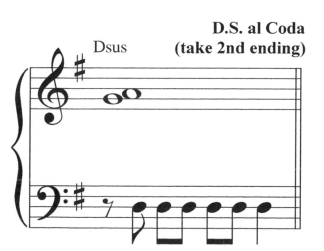

D.S. al Coda
(take 2nd ending)

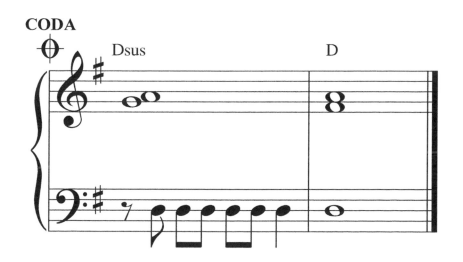

CODA

STEP BY STEP

Words and Music by
DAVID STRASSER "BEAKER"

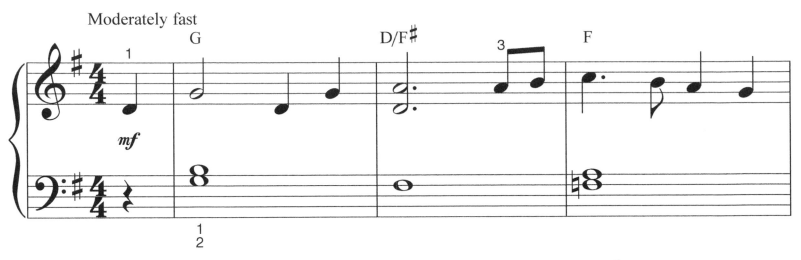

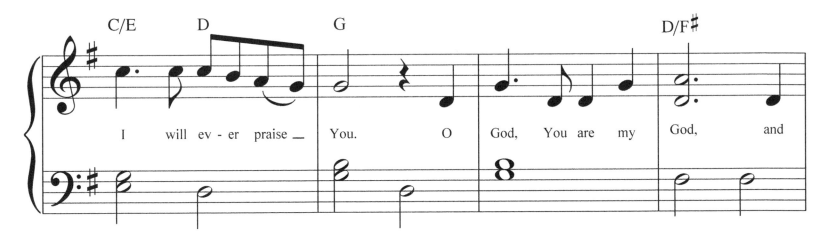

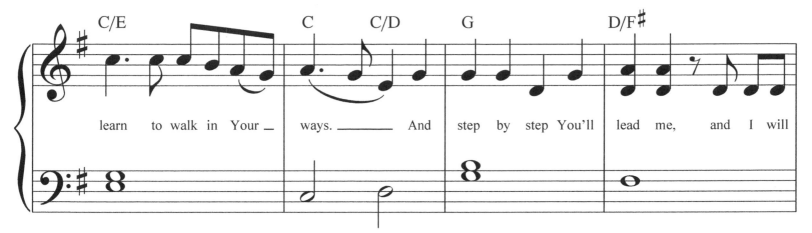

learn to walk in Your _ ways. _____ And step by step You'll lead me, and I will

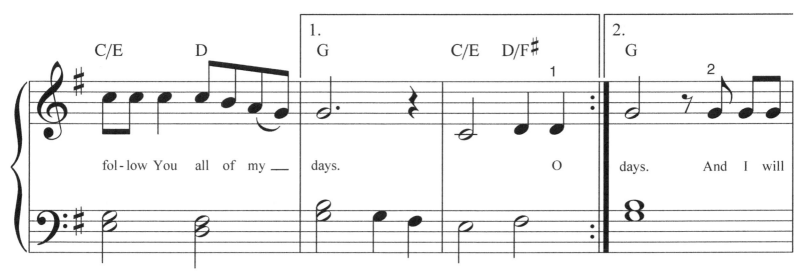

fol-low You all of my _ days. O days. And I will

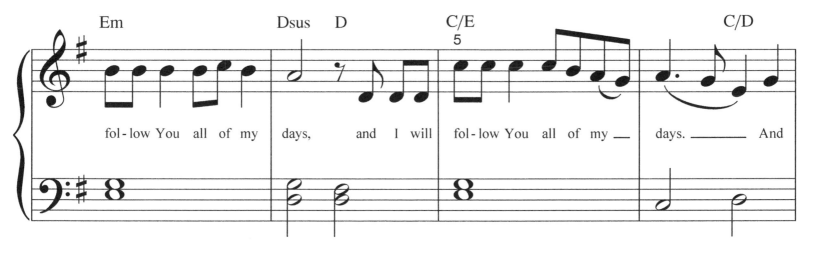

fol-low You all of my days, and I will fol-low You all of my _ days. _____ And

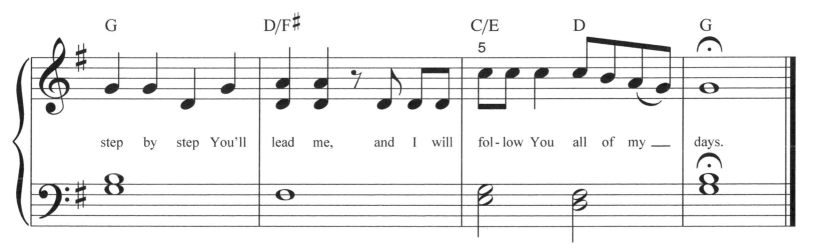

step by step You'll lead me, and I will fol-low You all of my _ days.

10,000 REASONS
(Bless the Lord)

Words and Music by JONAS MYRIN
and MATT REDMAN

Moderate Ballad

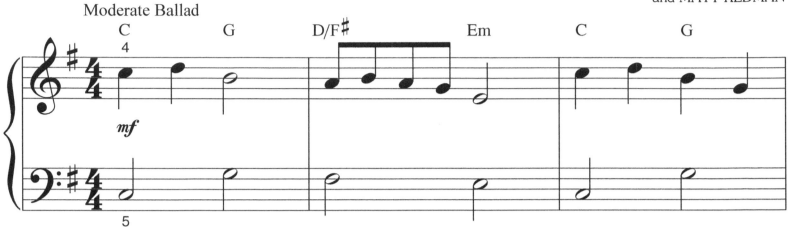

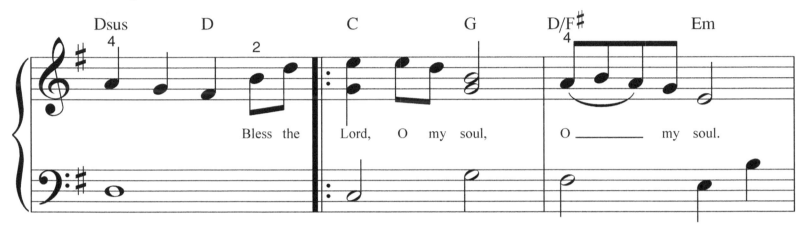

Bless the Lord, O my soul, O _____ my soul.

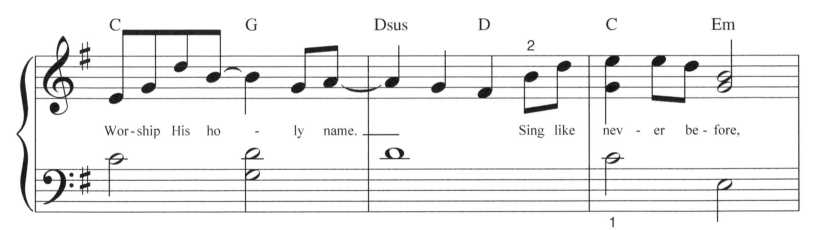

Wor-ship His ho - ly name. Sing like nev - er be - fore,

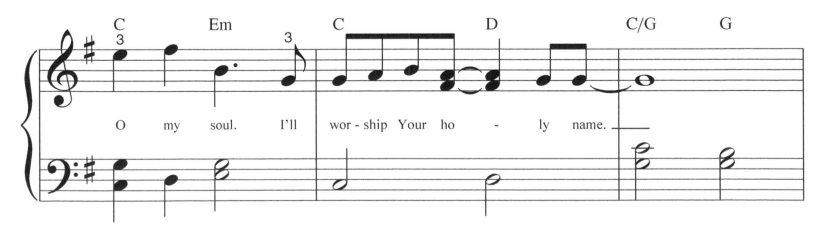

O my soul. I'll wor-ship Your ho - ly name.

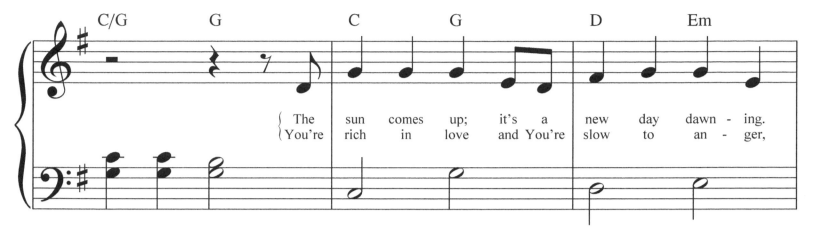

The sun comes up; it's a new day dawn-ing.
You're rich in love and You're slow to an - ger,

It's time to sing Your song a-gain. ___ What - ev-er may pass and what
Your name is great and Your heart is kind. ___ For all ___ Your good-ness I will

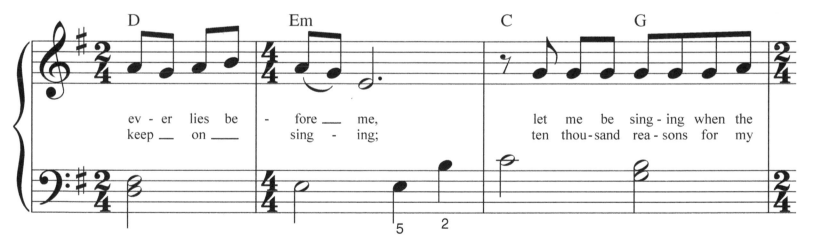

ev - er lies be - fore ___ me, let me be sing-ing when the
keep ___ on ___ sing - ing; ten thou-sand rea-sons for my

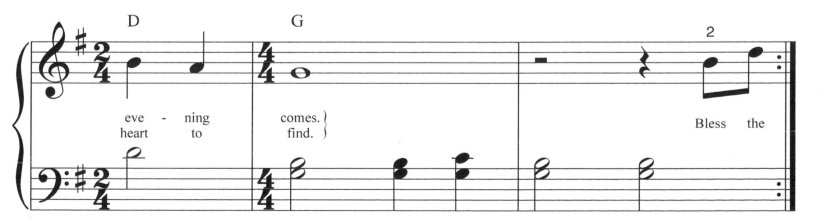

eve - ning comes.
heart to find.
Bless the

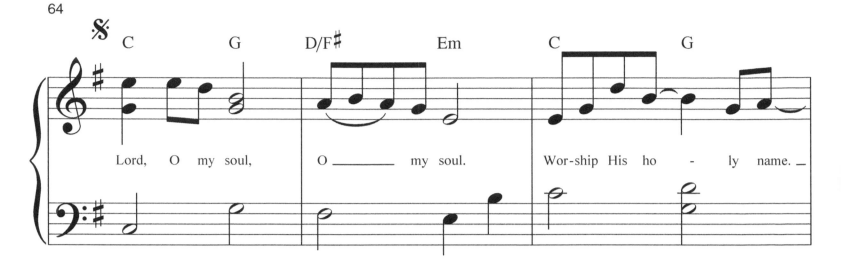

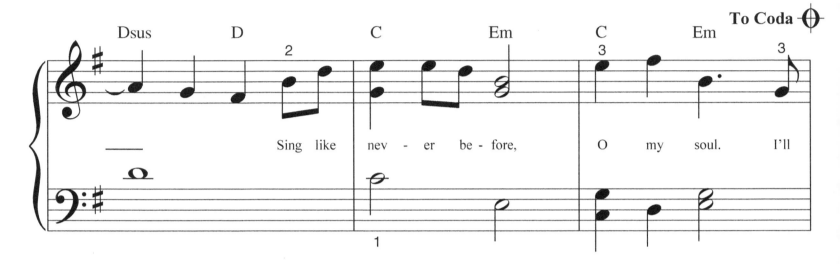

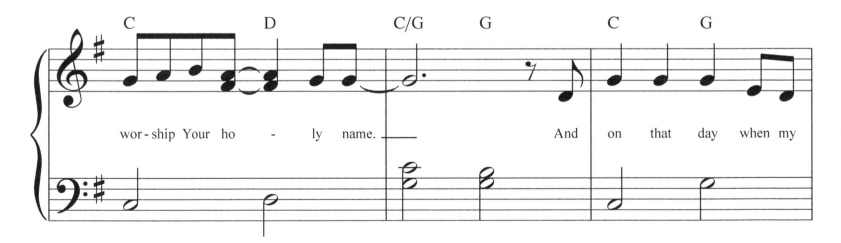

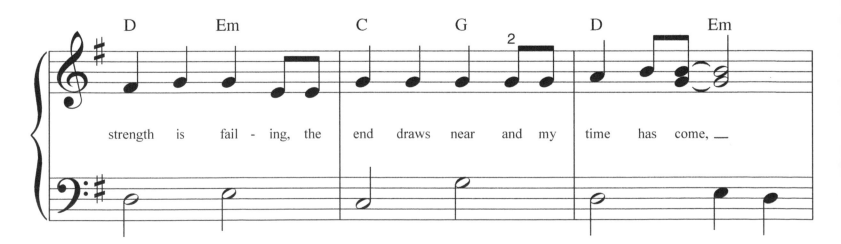

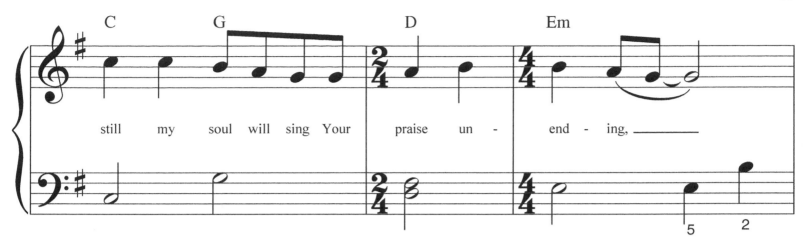

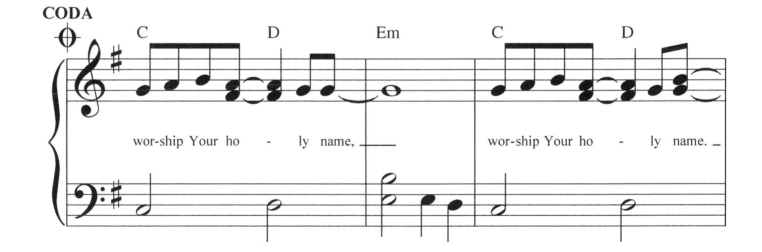

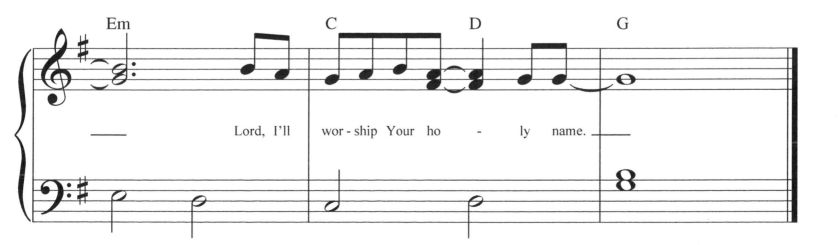

YOUR GRACE IS ENOUGH

Words and Music by
MATT MAHER

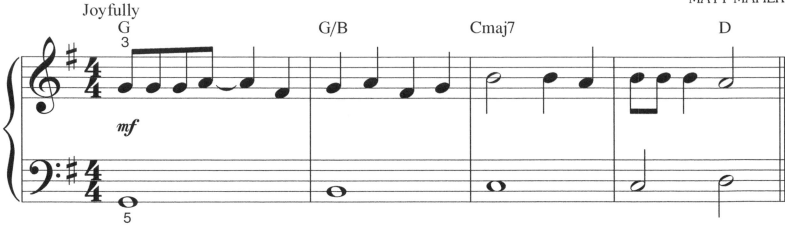

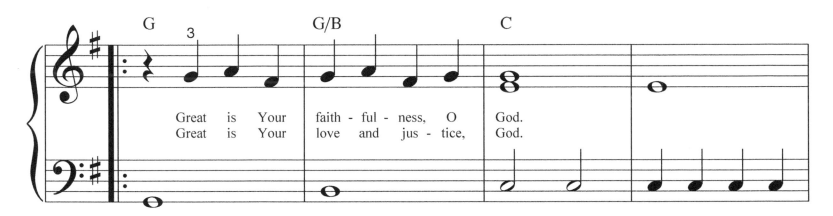

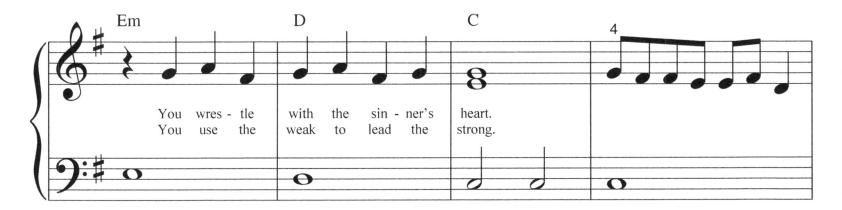

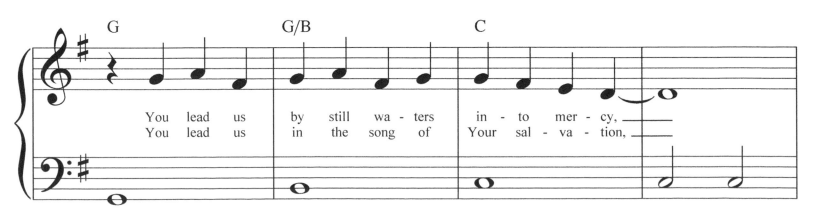

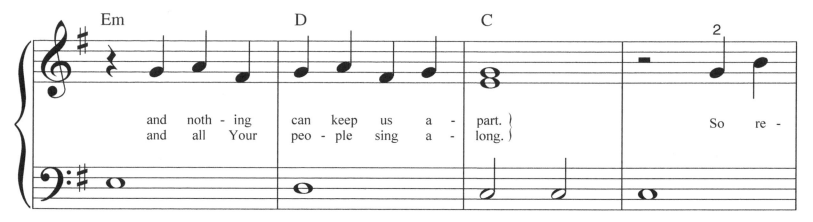

and noth - ing can keep us a - part.
and all Your peo - ple sing a - long.
So re -

mem - ber ___ Your peo - ple, ___ re - mem - ber ___ Your chil - dren, ___ re -

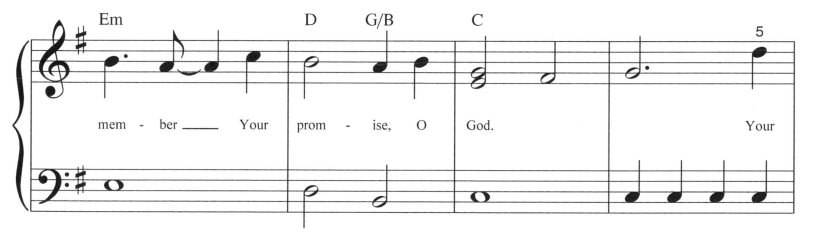

mem - ber ___ Your prom - ise, O God. Your

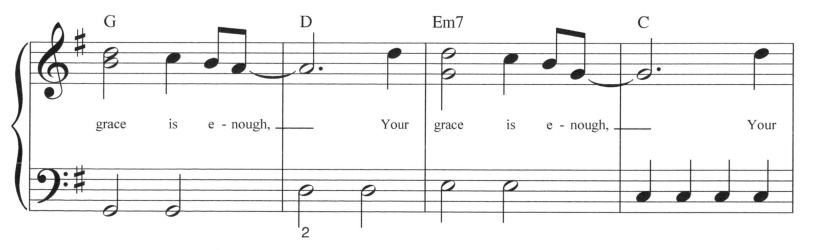

grace is e - nough, ___ Your grace is e - nough, ___ Your

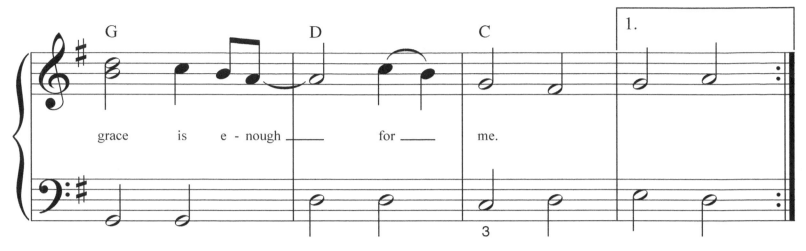

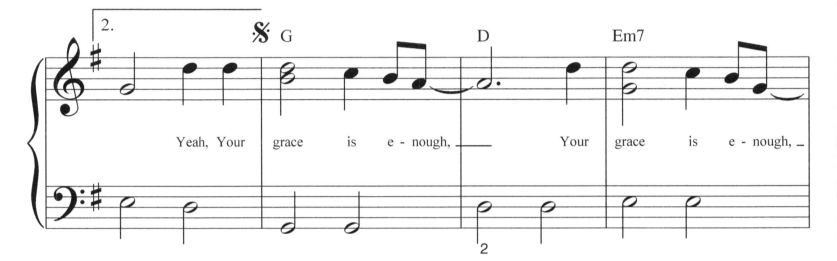

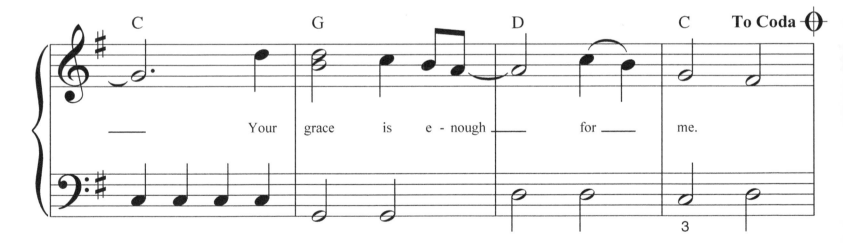

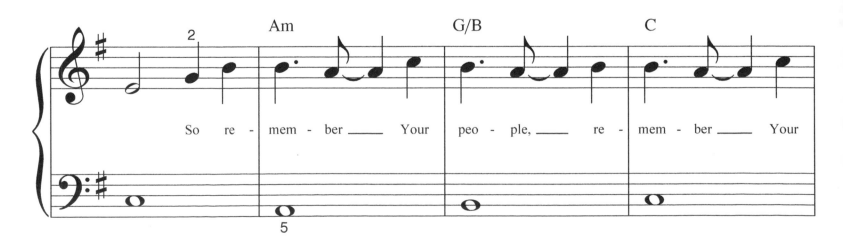

chil - dren, ____ re - mem - ber ____ Your prom - ise, O God.

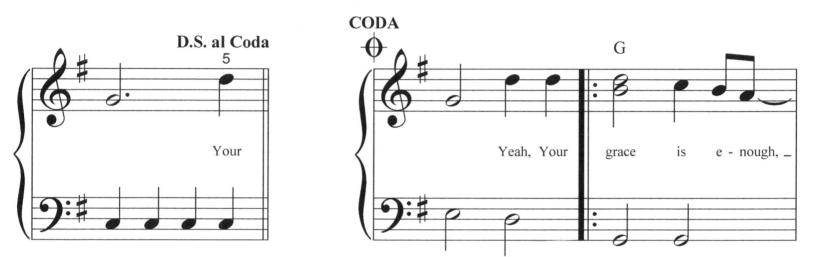

D.S. al Coda

Your

CODA

Yeah, Your grace is e - nough, _

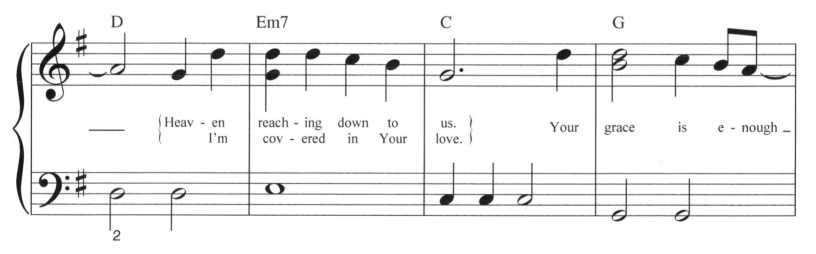

____ {Heav - en reach - ing down to us. } Your grace is e - nough _
I'm cov - ered in Your love. }

____ for ____ me, God, I see Your for ____ me.

YOUR NAME

Words and Music by PAUL BALOCHE
and GLENN PACKIAM

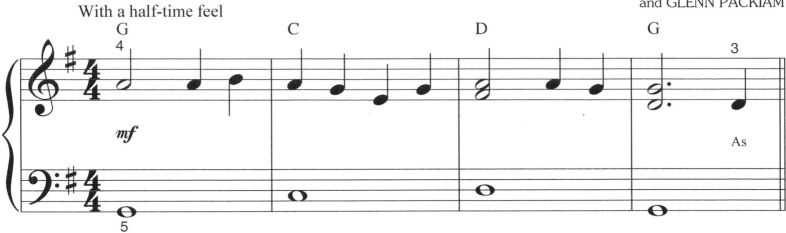

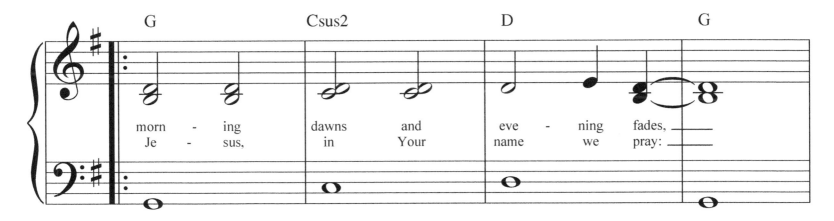

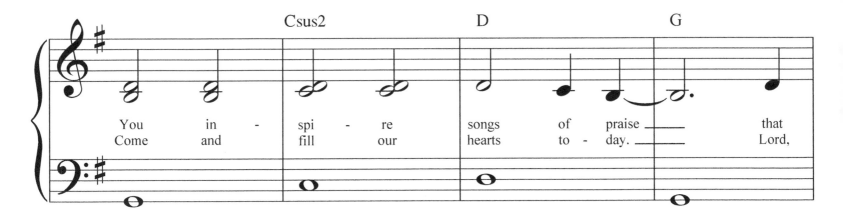

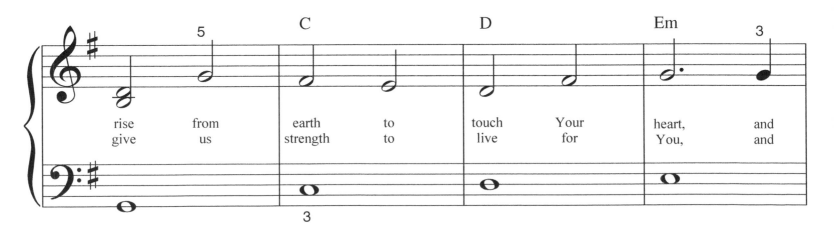

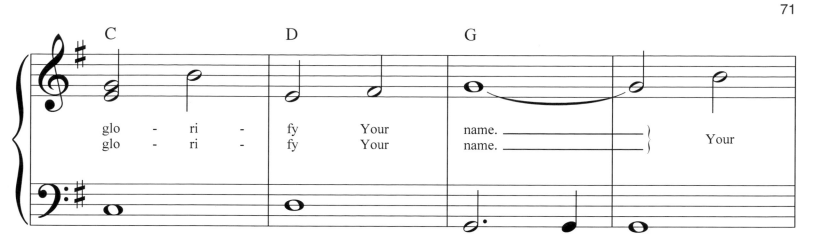

glo - ri - fy Your name. _____ Your
glo - ri - fy Your name. _____

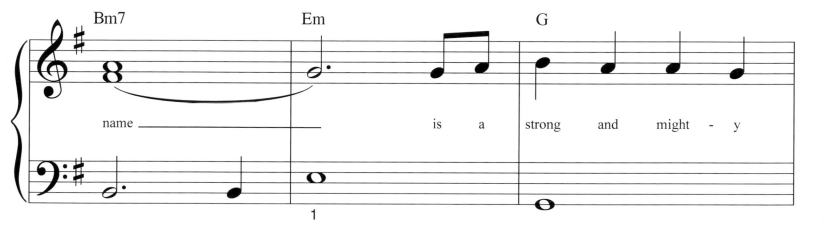

name _____ is a strong and might - y

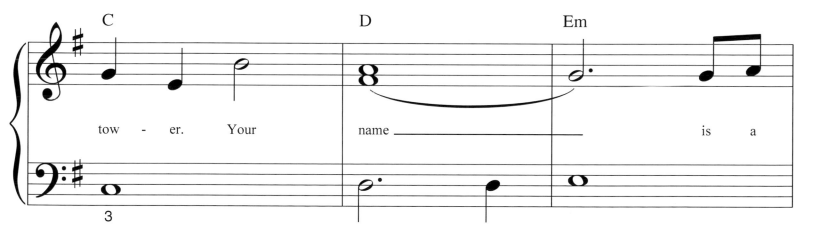

tow - er. Your name _____ is a

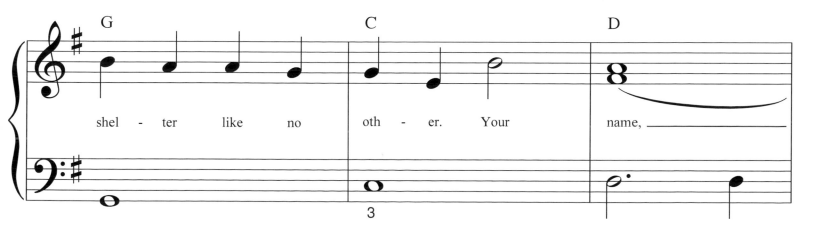

shel - ter like no oth - er. Your name, _____

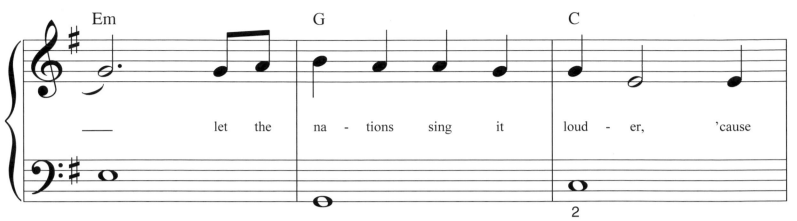

let the na - tions sing it loud - er, 'cause

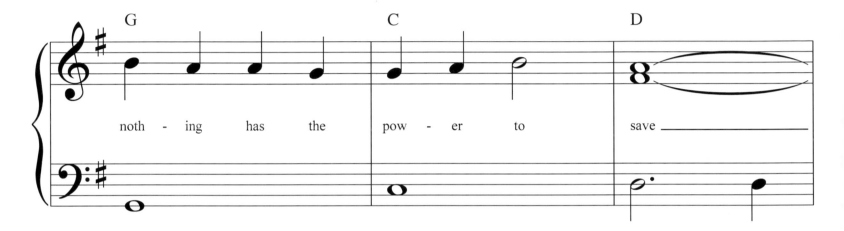

noth - ing has the pow - er to save _____

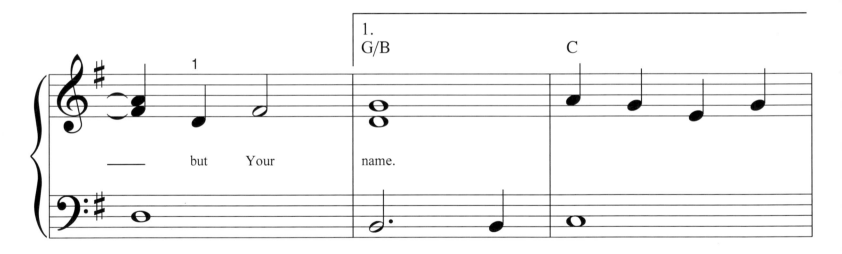

_____ but Your name.

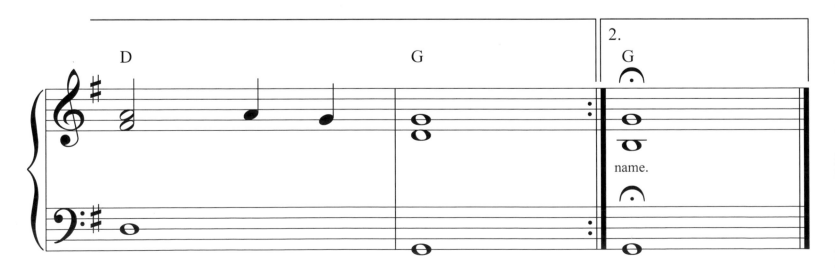

name.